Faces of Women and Aging

Faces of Women and Aging

Editors
Nancy D. Davis, MD
Ellen Cole, PhD
Esther D. Rothblum, PhD

The Haworth Press, Inc.
New York • London • Norwood (Australia)

Faces of Women and Aging has also been published as *Women & Therapy*, Volume 14, Numbers 1/2, 1993.

The Haworth Press, Inc., 10 Alice Street, Binghamton, NY 13904-1580 USA

Library of Congress Cataloging-in-Publication Data

Faces of women and aging / Nancy D. Davis, Ellen Cole, Esther D. Rothblum, editors.
    p. cm.
    "Also . . . published as Women & therapy, volume 14, numbers 1/2, 1993"-T.p. Verso.
    Includes bibliographical references.
    ISBN 1-56024-435-6 (hardback : acid-free paper).-ISBN 1-56023-042-8 (pbk. : acid-free paper)
    1. Middle aged women-Mental health. 2. Aged women-Mental health. 3. Middle aged women-Psychology. 4. Aged women-Psychology. 5. Aging-United States-Psychological aspects. 6. Ageism-United States. I. Davis, Nancy D. II. Cole, Ellen. III. Rothblum, Esther D.
RC451.4.M543F33 1993
155.6'6-dc20
                       93-6593
                       CIP

Faces of Women and Aging

CONTENTS

ABOUT THE EDITORS

Nancy D. Davis, M.D., has devoted 38 years to the practice of medicine first as an internist and later as a psychiatrist. Her interest in aging came from caring for older people where she learned to value their authentic approach to life. The examination of aging issues has become a passion for her as she herself approaches 65 and retirement from practice. She looks forward to more diversity in her life and becoming more authentic.

Ellen Cole, Ph.D., is a 52 year-old psychologist, director of the Master of Arts Program at Prescott College in Arizona, and the author and editor of numerous publications about human sexuality and women's mental health. She began to edit this collection thinking it was about other women. As the responses to the call for papers began to arrive, she was startled to see that many of them were about 50 year olds, suggesting of course that 50 was seen by others as falling with angst, laughter, and self-recognition.

Esther D. Rothblum, Ph.D., is Associate Professor in the Department of Psychology at the University of Vermont. She was the recipient of a Kellogg Fellowship that involved travel to Africa to study women's mental health. Her research and writing have focused on mental health disorders in which women predominate, including depression, the social stigma of women's weight, procrastination and fear of failure, and women in the Antarctic. She has co-edited eight books, including *Another Silenced Trauma: Twelve Feminist Therapists and Activists Respond to One Woman's Recovery from War* (co-edited with Ellen Cole), which won a Distinguished Publication Award from the Association for Women in Psychology.

Preface

We are pleased to devote the following pages to the subject of women and aging. We believe this is a timely and significant topic for women because old women are seen as poor, powerless, and pitiful in our sexist and youth-oriented society. The truth is that women age much more successfully than do men, who commit suicide with an ever-greater frequency as they age. Another truth is that women are increasingly in the majority as our population ages, and therefore women are increasingly in a position to assume more power. And accompanying this empowerment, the financial disadvantage which women, and especially old women, have endured has lessened (though, of course, far from disappeared).

Looking at aging from the point of view of the individual, we believe that middle and old age are merely stages of growth and development and not just seasons of loss and decline as the end approaches. Each life stage has its joys and sorrows; and old age, the last stage, has the joy of increasing self-knowledge and personal authenticity as the reward for the painful struggle of emotional growth in the face of the losses of aging.

We are proud that a number of our authors are themselves older women, and thus bring their own life experience and personality to the subject of aging. This is particularly true of the authors of the more personal and subjective articles in this collection. We have welcomed these personal stories, feeling they exemplify the diverse life experiences of women psychotherapists in their 50's, 60's, and 70's. Aging is always a uniquely personal experience.

We have placed the personal stories first, as a reminder that there is a human being behind every statistic and case study. We have placed them in roughly chronological order, by the age of the author who is telling her story. The subsequent articles are more theoretical and address some of the issues of aging in a more scientific format. We have arranged them chronologically, as well, according to the

xi

subject matter rather than the author's age. We are also pleased to note that these authors write about the aging process from very diverse points of view, thus exemplifying the complexity and individuality that characterize the many faces of women and aging.

We hope you enjoy reading this collection as much as we have enjoyed and profited from editing it.

Nancy D. Davis
Ellen Cole
Esther D. Rothblum

Late Mid-Life Astonishment:
Disruptions to Identity and Self-Esteem

Sarah F. Pearlman

SUMMARY. This paper describes and explores a developmental transition called "late mid-life astonishment." This transition or passage most typically begins between the ages of 50 and 60, is marked by a sudden awareness of the acceleration and stigmatization of aging, and characterized by feelings of amazement and despair at the convergence of diminished physical/sexual attractiveness and the multiple losses and changes brought about or occurring simultaneously with the increase of age. This transition then is a developmental crisis: one which can initiate a disruption of one's sense of self or identity and result in feelings of heightened vulnerability, shame, and severe loss of self-esteem. The paper concludes with implications for a psychotherapy which is validating of experience, attuned to the themes and tasks of late mid-life, and facilitating of the emergence of the personal resources necessary to confront and reconcile the reality of aging and discover its new and possible rewards.

There comes an age in everyone's life when you have to stand up straight and tall, look yourself straight in the mirror and say . . .What the hell happened here?

(American Greeting Card)

This paper is based on my own experience of growing older and the experiences and feelings related to me by Caucasian women

Sarah F. Pearlman, PsyD, received her doctorate in psychology at Antioch-New England Graduate School. She is currently in clinical practice in both Boston and Newburyport, MA and teaches courses in psychotherapy at Antioch-New England Graduate School and Lesley College.
The author thanks Norma Zacker for invaluable conversations–both serious and humorous on women and aging.

1

friends and students as well as clients (lesbian and heterosexual) –in both individual and group therapy in my clinical practice. My intent is to describe and explore a developmental transition or passage which I have labeled "late mid-life astonishment." While this paper will include discussion of a variety of changes and themes which tend to occur in late mid-life, its major focus will be on the experience of trauma and shame connected to a changed physical self.

This transition most typically begins between the ages of 50 and 60 and although there can be many initiating factors such as completion of menopause or declining health, it is triggered in many women by a sense of diminished physical/sexual attractiveness. The effect is a sudden awareness of the acceleration of aging characterized by feelings of amazement and despair at the recognition of multiple losses and changes brought about or occurring simultaneously with the increase of age. Late mid-life 'astonishment' is then a developmental crisis: one which can initiate a disruption of one's sense of self or identity and result in a severe loss of self-esteem accompanied by feelings of identity confusion, loss of confidence, heightened vulnerability, depression, and growing feelings of shame and self-consciousness focused on physical appearance.

While the mid-life years are often the span of time when many women achieve an increased sense of self and confidence in their abilities, later mid-life signals a next and unwanted turning point. What differentiates this transition from earlier mid-life is the traumatizing experience of a different physical self and the awareness that one indeed is approaching the entry point of old age. Thus, although all of the mid-life years comprise a transition, each end possesses its own distinctiveness and cannot be collapsed into one uniform or identical developmental era.

Unlike younger mid-life women, the late mid-life woman finds that "passing" as younger is no longer possible, that losses or changes in health and sexuality are now a reality, and that lack of social interest on the part of younger people has become an increasingly common experience. Early mid-life may be the theory, but late mid-life is the practice–with a notable difference between theorizing about the experience of aging and the actual experience or "lived practice" of becoming older.

THE POLITICS OF AGE:
MEDIA EXPLOITATIONS/ACCELERATING FEARS

Around five years ago, I picked up a women's fashion magazine and was amazed to find page after page devoted to advertisements of skin creams and other treatment products promising both the prevention of aging and/or the return to a more youthful appearance. At the time, I was managing to maintain a rather grandiose and arrogant fantasy that aging happened to other women–a fantasy buttressed by an ultra-feminist consciousness which I believed lent immunity to media hype and mainstream social norms on youthful looks. I continued to view ageism, weightism, and looksism as patriarchal politics, and had convinced myself that through the fortunate combination of personal/political strength of character and good genes (I had a remarkably young looking mother), I would never succomb to the lure of make-overs and night creams. Moreover, as a lesbian, I believed that I did not need to be concerned with meeting the prescribed appearance standards of men and that my life span of physical attractiveness (and attractiveness to women) would extend well past that of the majority of heterosexual women.

These convictions were reinforced by writings (Doress & Siegel, 1987) which focused on information[1] on menopause and other health concerns and emphasized the rewards of aging in order to empower women–as well a sequence of pot luck birthday celebrations which conveyed the status of crone on women turning 40. Although I tended to avoid workshops on aging at women's conferences, I did read Barbara MacDonald's (1983) and Baba Copper's (1988) books on aging and their experiences and reactions to changes in physical appearance, trivialization, and social avoidance by others. However, these themes did not seem to be personally relevant.

The truth was that I had not yet reached late mid-life.

In addition, until my enlightening acquaintance with this particu-

---

1. This is not meant to devalue information, nor to deny the rewards of aging, or denigrate the importance of symbols and a spirituality which honors aspects of femaleness and age. My point is that without the balance of validation of the difficulties involved in aging, denial of ageism is fostered and the experience of aging in women trivialized.

lar fashion magazine, I had not been aware of the acceleration of the skin product industry–nor of the increase in obsessive concern with retaining youthful looks. Nor did I realize that what I had stumbled upon was the extremely successful exploitation (age terrorism) of women's fears of growing older which Naomi Wolf (1991) calls the media construction of the "sin of aging" (p. 95). To Wolf, this exploitation is aimed directly at women's fears of real and imaginary wrinkles connected to fears of age discrimination, being passed over in the workplace, and rejection or abandonment by romantic partners or mates.

Moreover, Wolf suggests that as more and more women left the domestic sphere for the workplace, media advertising could no longer successfully focus on home care products to produce the perfect home. Thus, a marketing vacuum was created and advertising turned to female consumers with the mythological promise that every woman could take control and attain perfect looks and a perfect body.

In addition, both Wolf (1991) and Susan Faludi (1991) offer an extremely compelling explanation for this facet of the recent politics of aging. These authors connect new and powerful social rules on female appearance (youthful and thin good looks) manifested by media exploitation of women's fear of aging to a backlash against women originating in arousal of male gender insecurities and psychological fears of women's freedom. This backlash originated as a reaction to an historically specific period (the 60's and 70's) which was characterized by an unprecedented sequence of political protest (Black civil rights, the anti-Vietnam war movement, women's liberation and gay liberation movements) and joined to a personal, sexual, and de-genderizing quest for liberation.

It was an era which initiated new appearance codes (dress, hair) among young people; an era which threatened to change traditional feminine/masculine roles and defied mainstream gender imperatives as well as male imposed and evaluated standards of beauty which defined acceptable femininity. Men grew their hair long; women discarded make-up and stopped shaving legs and armpits. In addition, the lesbian feminist and gay male liberation movements resulted in an increased homosexual visibility and many lesbians adopted a casual or masculinized ethos of dress, which Loulan

(1991) calls the "androgynous imperative" (p. 11), therefore inten-sifying sexual ambiguity and further extending the limits of gender. In response to these threats to male dominance, privilege, and the established gender order, the backlash which emerged established through media images a more demanding criteria for gender-based esteem and feminine success at work and in relationships, thus reinstating traditional feminine appearance norms. These criteria were both created and reinforced by a media which began to present extreme images of the female young, thin, and the extraordinarily good-looking–as well as to censor how women, particularly older women really look (Wolf, 1991). Media images seeped into both female and male psyche and a new and stricter visual sensibility and standard was created, defining what women should look like, what men should desire, and what men should feel entitled to.

These exacting standards and images served then to insure a more profound stigmatization of aging and that women (both les-bian and heterosexual) would suffer chronic doubts as to physical attractiveness. In addition, they promoted increasing concern over loss of youthful looks which began to emerge at increasingly youn-ger ages (Brownmiller, 1984). These images functioned then to preoccupy and punish women; to create a wall of separation be-tween younger and older women; to contain and terminate newly won freedoms; erode liberating beliefs and behaviors, and deflect women away from political analysis and action–thus countering the gains and promise of the women's revolution.

LATE MID-LIFE ASTONISHMENT

Most women will struggle from adolescence onwards to maintain a sense of self-worth against this backdrop of social rules and media images of female appearance. However, it is the physical changes of late mid-life which signals the beginning of old age and presents a particular vulnerability to disruptions of identity and self-esteem. Specifically, the more a woman has relied upon her youthful looks, based her identity on her physical/sexual attractiveness, and rooted her sense of self and self-esteem in her appearance, the greater her vulnerability to changes in her physical self–and the greater the loss and assault upon self-esteem.

What many late mid-life women report is a leap in awareness of diminished physical/sexual attractiveness (socially defined) with resulting feelings of astonishment at what seems to be a remarkably sudden change. Confirmed by mirrors and photographs, these new reflections are fundamentally at odds with the woman's self-image and the person she wishes to look like. Women relate feelings of emotional shock at the cumulative effect of graying hair, deepening wrinkles, coarsening skin texture, and increase in facial hair. In addition, features seem to alter as facial lines begin to engrave expressions of harshness, unhappiness, or dissatisfaction which Brownmiller (1984) attributes to the normal downward pull of gravity.

As one woman expressed it: "I used to look in the mirror and see myself . . . now I see my mother." And, another. "I feel as if I look out at the world from behind my face. My face feels the same, but when I look in the mirror, it's an older woman who stares back at me. I always liked the way I looked and sought out mirrors for the pleasure of looking at myself. Now I hate mirrors. I feel better when I just feel and don't look."

However, to MacDonald (1983), women who refuse to see themselves and re-orient to a changing self make a pact or collude with denial.

Also, the normal transformation of women's bodies at menopause brings about weight gain as well as shifts in body weight which result in thickening about the waist and increase of abdominal fat (Voda, Christy & Morgan, 1991). Thus, mid-life women can be bewildered and appalled by their new and heavier bodies and the sudden understanding that they may no longer have the physiological ability to lose weight and to maintain the body of a young woman, and that their bodies are no longer under their control in a world which worships control.

As one woman exclaimed: "I looked in the mirror and I couldn't see my behind! I figured maybe it just moved and settled about my middle . . . and that I needed to mark this day down somewhere . . . the day I lost my behind. Then I began to laugh. I mean . . . you definitely need humor about all of this."

Many late mid-life women confirm Copper's (1988) perceptions of the stigmatization of age and that somewhere in the 50's there is an acceleration of social invisibility, inattention, and rejection. To Copper, younger women are unwilling to identify with women older than themselves (which led her to conclude that mid-life woman can no longer be identified as an ally of the elderly). Siegel (1990) observes also that younger women are often rejecting or distancing to older women in women's organizations. In addition, invisibility often takes the form (in both lesbian and heterosexual women) of no longer being sexually noticed by men, an ambivalent experience of feeling protected from unwanted male attention and objectification, yet missing this acknowledgement of one's sexual attractiveness.

To MacDonald (1983), when a woman is no longer viewed by others as young and desirable, she begins a struggle to retain a sense of self in the face of new and distressing perceptions by others that declare she is old. Both Brownmiller (1984) and Posin (1991) describe feelings of failure and guilt connected to aging, as if one has done something wrong–or hasn't done enough. Indeed, some women speak of feeling betrayed, stating that they did all the right things–avoided sun, ate healthful foods, took vitamins, and exercised–and still they aged.

These experiences are painful confirmations to the woman in late mid-life that she is indeed older and that she no longer meets the social criteria of a physically and sexually attractive woman. For many late mid-life women, the loss of socially defined attractiveness is severely disruptive to self-concept and a traumatizing assault upon healthy narcissism: that is one's feelings of self-love and self-worth. When self-love and self-worth are diminished, the result is the activation of shame–as if becoming/looking older means that something is deeply and truly wrong with oneself. In addition, women often experience a secondary shame which is based in beliefs that these reactions are neurotic, superficial, and vain. Companions to shame are depression, loss of confidence, increasing self-consciousness about one's changed physical appearance, and anxiety in social situations which is reinforced by incidents of invisibility and rejection.

Moreover, social anxiety can provoke withdrawal and increased isolation resulting in loss of relational connections, and in single women, the potential for new friends and partners. These feelings of anxiety and self-consciousness are often intensified in situations such as reunions or other gatherings where the woman has not seen certain friends or acquaintances for an extended period of time (as if changes in physical appearance are less apparent if one is seen on a more consistent basis). Indeed, one woman reported feeling traumatized when a woman whom she had not seen for 12 years failed to recognize her.

To lesbians, prior meeting places such as gay bars or lesbian social or professional events may no longer seem socially comfortable due to heightened feelings of difference and comparison with younger women. Finally, for both lesbians and heterosexual women, social withdrawal and loss of social resources will intensify the risk of severe depression–and also solitary drinking and alcoholism in women who are vulnerable to substance dependency.

An additional area of confusion and surprise which reinforces the experience of aging are changes in sexuality and responsivity such as decrease in sexual desire which in earlier mid-life may have seemed inconceivable (Cole, 1988). Reduced vaginal lubrication which typically follows menopause may mean that wetness will no longer signal the beginning of desire. The thinning of vaginal walls can restrict sexual play (digital and dildo stimulation) in lesbian sex and cause heterosexual intercourse to become painful. In addition, many women find that reaching orgasm takes longer (not always a disadvantage) or that decrease in intensity of orgasm is frustrating and disappointing. Also, self-consciousness about appearance and weight gain can function to reduce sexual desire and sexual frequency.

Changes in health, typical in late mid-life, are often a traumatizing confirmation of aging, especially to women who have defined themselves through perfect health, high energy, and active life styles. Common conditions such as arthritis, hypertension, increasingly poor night vision, and loss of hearing challenge many late mid-life woman to adjust to new limitations and to continue activity although sustaining chronic physical discomfort. In addition, normal cognitive changes which affect memory and immediate recall (although often referred to with humor) can cause frustration as well as concern. Finally, changes in health status tend to connect to fears of future incapacitating illness, loss of independence, and inability to work and eventual poverty, especially in women who are self-supporting.

Reactions to changes in physical appearance, sexuality, and health in late mid-life are also affected by partnership status. Both lesbians and heterosexual woman who are single can be fearful that they will no longer be able to attract a potential mate while lesbians express concern that they tend to be attracted to younger women who are no longer attracted to them (the effectiveness of media images). Heterosexual women who are partnered frequently express insecurities that their mate will lose interest and leave for a younger woman–concerns which are certainly grounded in statistics and observations of current heterosexual marital/divorce patterns.

In addition, late mid-life is often the age when women are confronted with the responsibility of caring for aging parents and/or when one experiences the death of parents and other older family members. This heightens awareness of how quickly time passes, that life is finite, and that one indeed is the next generation and has reached the border of advancing age.

Finally, similar to earlier life transitions, late-mid-life frequently calls forth self-scrutiny and evaluation of one's current life situation and life choices. Indeed, late mid-life in many women appears to confer both the ability and the willingness to examine oneself more deeply and gain additional new insights–insights which can illuminate personality struggles and their painful connection to past choices, behaviors, and interactions which have contributed to difficult or terminated relationships and lack of desired achievements.

In one women's words: "I've much fewer friends than I'd like. I've left a lot of people without telling them why. I was always able to find some fault with them to explain why they disappointed me. Except now I realize that I expected everyone to be how I wanted . . . and if they weren't . . . well I'd just get so angry . . . and I didn't see that I wasn't so easy to get along with myself. I never did see that my actions caused their actions."

To women who have mothered, late mid-life can initiate an era of rewarding relationships with adult children as well as the joys of grandmothering a child. However, that mothers are responsible for the personality outcome of their children is pervasive ideology. When mothers observe the problems and struggles of their adult children, they often attribute these problems to deficits in mothering. Thus, many mothers of grown children become preoccupied by feelings of regret and remorse: that is regrets connected to earlier mothering and times of insensitivity, neglect, or lack of interest in their young child and/or not adequately protecting their child from an abusive and/or alcoholic mate or husband.

The consequences of maternal remorse can be relationships with adult children which are shaped by guilt, ambivalence, and inappropriate behaviors as if to make amends for adult children's problems. Guilt invites feelings of inappropriate obligation and thus exploitation of mothers by children. It prevents the setting of limits on insensitive or abusive behaviors on the part of grown children and inhibits appropriate expectations such as mutuality of caring, giving, and respect. In addition, it hinders adult children from seeing their mother as a separate person and can keep (and protect) women from focusing on their own lives.

IMPLICATIONS FOR PSYCHOTHERAPY WITH LATE MID-LIFE WOMEN

Similar to other socially stigmatized identity transitions (Pearlman, in press), increased acceptance of aging is a process of re-occurring and over-lapping reactions and struggles. These include phases of denial; recognition; comparison to oneself as younger (and to younger women); increasing tolerance; and finally re-conceptualization of identity, and reconciliation and acceptance of the reality of aging–and oneself as older.

These phases can serve as guidelines and shape a clinical approach which is attuned to the prevalent issues of late mid-life and which validates, normalizes, and enables reconciliation of the multiple losses and traumas connected to the increase of age. Therapy, therefore can encourage the late mid-life woman to express distress over changes in physical appearance and to disclose feelings of shame. In addition, it can assist her with coming to terms with past choices and regrets such as decreasing guilt and maternal remorse over perceived mothering deficits through focusing on maternal strengths and attending to her current relationship with her adult children.

Therapists may need to focus on sources of anxiety and depression in late mid-life clients and utilize approaches which help decrease behaviors such as social withdrawal as well as encourage social risk taking in order to increase social connection. Moreover, it is imperative that therapists become knowledgeable about community resources for health and sexuality concerns as well as social/emotional resources such as groups for older women where their experiences can be validated in an environment of commonality and supports.

Critical to maintaining a positive self-concept in spite of the stigmatization of aging are those rewards and reinforcements which determine life style happiness and contentment. For single women, these rewards can be self-determination, freedom of choice, and the joys of solitude and varied relationships. For partnered women, there are the multiple rewards of a primary relationship. Overall, it appears that the most stable foundations for the acceptance of aging and thus the goals of late mid-life include the following: personal life style rewards such as meaningful work and interests; social support; affiliation and belonging; positive role models; spirituality, political understanding of the oppression of older people, and engaging in social/political activism on behalf of older people.[2]

Finally, my experience of late mid-life is that it is indeed possible to pass through the 'astonishment' transition, regain the emotional balance and self-assuredness of one's earlier mid-life years, and in addition, gain in inner directedness, self-acceptance, and acceptance of one's current life. Yet, social rules on attractiveness and sexual desirability are powerful cultural adversaries and acceptance of aging in all probability will be accompanied by the occasional re-surfacing of residual sadness and regrets that one is no longer young. There are harsh realities to aging and these feelings can be easily triggered by episodes of rejection and invisability, reminders of physical limitaitons and other losses, and/or nostaigic recall of the escapades of one's younger years.

Future struggles and adjustments to growing older and age stigmatization clearly loom ahead. However, if the tasks of 'astonishment' have been accomplished, these struggles can be met with courage and humor–as well as with legitimate anger and indignation.

---

2. To these I would add the importance of some sense of security that financial and health care needs will be adequately met.

REFERENCES

Brownmiller, S. (1984). *Femininity*. NY: Ballantine Books.

Cole, E. (1988). Sex at menopause: Each in her own way. *Women & Therapy, 7*, (2/3), 159-168.

Copper, B. (1988). *Over the hill: Reflections on ageism between women*. Freedom, CA: The Crossing Press.

Doress, P., & Siegel, D. (Eds.) (1988). *Ourselves growing older: Women aging with knowledge and power*. NY: Simon and Schuster.

Faludi, S. (1991). *Backlash: The undeclared war against American women*. NY: Crown Publishers.

Loulan, J. (1991). "Now when I was your age": One perspective on how lesbian culture has influenced our sexuality. In B. Sang, J. Warshaw, & A. Smith (Eds.), *Lesbians at midlife: The creative transition* (pp. 10-18). San Francisco: Spinsters Book Co.

MacDonald, C. (1983). *Look me in the eye: Old women, aging and ageism*. San Francisco: Spinsters/Aunt Lute.

Pearlman, S. (in press). Heterosexual mothers/lesbian daughters: Parallels and similarities. *Journal of Feminist Family Therapy*.

Posin, R. (1991). Ripening. In B. Sang, J., Warshaw, & A. Smith (Eds.), *Lesbians at midlife: The creative transition* (pp. 143-146). San Francisco: Spinsters Book Co.

Siegel, R. J. (1990). Old women as mother figures. *Women & Therapy, 10* (1/2), 71-96.

Voda, A., Christy, N. & Morgan, J. (1991). Body composition changes in menopausal women. *Women & Therapy, 11* (2), 89-97.

Wolf, N. (1991). *The beauty myth: How images of beauty are used against women*. NY: William Morrow & Co.

When Mary Stopped Talking

Sarah B. Nelson

SUMMARY. This is an intimate account of my relationship with my sister after she experienced a sudden, unexpected, and massive stroke at age 62, two years ago. In the telling of this story I hope to provide readers/therapists with an increased understanding of the two clinical conditions, aphasia and apraxia. I also hope to heighten awareness not only of the day-to-day, but also of the inner experiences of such patients and their family members. As a sister and a psychiatrist, I have had a unique opportunity to learn from this family tragedy. I would like to pass on my observations to others who will inevitably be relating as therapists or as relatives to stroke patients and their families as our population ages. Although this is simply one clinical vignette, readers may take from it whatever is relevant to their own life or practice.

Ask me "How's your sister?" and I will find it very difficult to stop talking about Mary. Her situation is so unusual, so painfully frustrating, yet so inspiring, that I feel compelled to try to explain with a rush of words and gestures and even mimicry to anyone who seems at all interested.

Imagine, if you can, waking up in a world both familiar and confusing. You are unable not only to use your right arm and right leg, but worse, unable to communicate your thoughts, feelings, or even basic needs by words or gestures. Imagine your native language seeming like a foreign language, with the sounds, the written letters, and the enunciation impossible for you to comprehend or

Sarah B. Nelson, MD, is a 67 year old Psychiatrist in private practice in Phoenix, AZ. Formerly a family doctor in Pennsylvania, her current areas of special interest include dysfunctional mind-body relationships and teaching about and leading small psychodynamic out-patient groups. She feels privileged to serve as mentor to younger colleagues.

13

reproduce. Imagine having been a bright, educated leader in your community, then being unable to call your husband by his name. Imagine not being able to say your own name when asked to do so.

Two years ago at age 62, my sister Mary had a massive left cerebral stroke. When she awoke from the coma, she had a complete right hemiplegia and a profound aphasia and apraxia. What this meant functionally was that her right arm and right leg were paralyzed; she could not speak, read or write; she could not make any purposeful, meaningful gestures. Yet she was alert, she obviously experienced pain and pleasure, and she clearly had a limited understanding of the conversations and actions of those around her, which she communicated by spontaneous facial expressions, smiles, grimaces, or frowns. She laughed appropriately and ate enthusiastically whatever she was fed.

In the early days and weeks, Mary's husband and I were given hope from stories of others who had made remarkable recoveries "after the swelling goes down . . . in a few hours . . . days . . . weeks." The only physician in the family, I kept to myself my terrible recurring thought: "She'll never be able to talk again."

Physiotherapy and speech therapy were pursued rigorously during her three-month hospital stay. Gradually, though awkwardly, she began to feed herself with her left hand. She was slowly trained to walk with a brace and a cane. Two facts became increasingly apparent. One was that Mary was an unusual patient in her drive to learn and to progress, and in her unfailing good spirits. Everyone who worked with her benefited from her joyous attitude and energy. The second more slowly accepted fact was that the damage to the left side of her brain had been severe and extensive.

Mary and I are only 3 years apart. I am older, now 67. We have a younger sister, now 57, but because of the age difference, Carol has not joined in Mary's and my sisterly bond. Mary and I spent our childhoods together. We'd ride our bikes to secret picnic areas in the woods where we chewed sassafras, cooked bacon over a forbidden fire, and argued over the penny candy we bought with ten cents from our allowances. Mary would save her money and savor her chocolate ice cream slowly, whereas I would spend all my money and gobble my vanilla ice cream too fast.

Grown up and married with three children each, we visited back and forth between Pennsylvania and New Jersey comparing recipes, sharing birthdays and holidays, and playing competitive bridge as a foursome with our husbands. I went to medical school and became a family doctor and later a psychiatrist. Mary studied the humanities and became a leader in various civic activities. She campaigned for fluoridation in her town and against drugs in the high school. She obtained a Masters degree in Human Sexuality, and she and her husband taught sex education to adolescents. I have always envied her social skills, whereas she has tended to idealize me as the older, 'wiser' professional sister. We've been different but close. My family moved to Phoenix, Arizona in 1972. Seven years later Mary and her husband Peter followed.

When my friends learned that Mary could not speak, they wanted to be helpful. They kept making suggestions. Why didn't we make written signs for her? Or give her a pencil and paper? Or get her to point or do sign language?

I tried to explain the condition of apraxia to them. Apraxia means an inability to make purposeful, meaningful movements. Imagine wanting a tissue or a blanket and not being able even to pantomime the act of sniffing or shivering. Mary could not form a glass shape with her uninvolved left hand and lift it to her lips to indicate a need for a drink of water. With profound apraxia and without any paralysis or other defect, a person cannot, of her own volition nor on command, perform ordinary simple actions. Mary could not smile, point, or make a fist on purpose. Therefore, even with intact intelligence, there was no possibility of clear communication by the use of body movements or symbolization at that time.

Mary could spontaneously smile, grimace, and move in response to emotion or other stimuli. She could eat and learned to feed herself early because eating and feeding behaviors are largely instinctive. Eating has always been a special pleasure to my sister and has continued to be so after her stroke. She never puts an extra pound on her small, slender frame, but she does enjoy her meals. Some of our best communication was–and still is–done through food.

Speech therapy began with humming, teaching Mary to form an "M" sound. This was difficult for her. It was also painful for me and others in our family to watch as these lessons proceeded. "M" was combined with the vowels to form "ma . . me . . mi . . mo . . mu," all slowly, repetitively, a struggle. Mary learned by watching how the speech therapist formed the sounds with her lips and tongue. This is called "cueing." It was arduous and tedious work. My sister remained eager and pleasant, responding to small successes with gleeful laughs. After three months insurance payments for such therapy stopped, but therapy was continued because of Mary's high motivation and the family's hopefulness and support. After six months she could enunciate many words fairly clearly, but only with cueing.

She was elated. Nevertheless, the truth was that she could only mimic speech. However, by this time she had such an emotional investment in speech therapy and such an emotional bond with the very supportive therapist that Mary insisted on continuing the lessons. Her husband could not say no to her. The speech therapist was direct about the possibility of wasting the families' resources and honest in her appraisal of her patient's limited chance for much future gain. We all decided to go on, nevertheless, recognizing that perhaps the major gains would be psychotherapeutic.

Today, after more than two years of speech therapy, Mary still has no functional speech. She cannot initiate words without watching someone else say the word, or very occasionally, on hearing the word. To this day, she cannot call to her husband, saying "Peter." She cannot produce her own name voluntarily and unaided. She cannot ask in words for a drink, a tissue, a sweater, or the bathroom.

The apraxia has improved considerably, however, and today Mary can make more directed gestures and symbols. She can also write a few words. She has improved her reading and math skills through working with a graduated computerized reading program. This is so important to a woman who used to read the Wall Street Journal, kept voluminous files on stocks and mutual funds, and was the former President of the Board of a prestigious museum. However, her main means of communication is still by vocalizations with expressive variations and by the use of six words I will explain more about soon. One of her frequent paths for communication is by use of the repetitious nonsense syllables, "Sa . . Soon . . Sa . . Soon . . Sa . . Soon . . " with which she can tell a whole story. If the listener is smart enough, and tuned in to her, he or she may be able to get the gist of it.

Almost from the beginning it was clear that there was a mind inside that damaged brain, and a personality much like that of the pre-stroke Mary. However, like most gravely ill people, Mary was for a while quite egocentric and insecure. She was rigidly controlling and panicked in the face of change. She was surprisingly dependent. Prior to her stroke, Mary had always taken care of herself and others. She had been a very bright, and capable perfectionist. She was also socially perceptive and a lovely hostess. Her enthusiasm and expressiveness were endearing. Now, as she improves from her stroke she continues to be all these things despite her terrible handicaps. She gives the impression of being herself by greeting newcomers with a joyful "Hi" (one of her first and few words), by listening attentively, by smiling and laughing responsively, and by looking quizzical. She has also learned to say "bye" and "no" and "yes."

The rest of Mary's conversation is carried on through the use of two words that evolved spontaneously. The two words are "Oh boy." It is hard to believe how much an expressive person can convey by altering the tone, inflection and pacing of the two words "Oh boy." When excited or pleased, she will say "Oh boy . . Oh boy . . Oh boy!" in rapid-fire enthusiasm. When distressed or sad, she will say "Oh boy" anxiously or "Oh boy" slowly with pathos. Her intent is often clear. Seven months post-stroke Mary attended a Fourth of July party after which one of the guests marveled that he had never seen anyone who could say so much with just two words.

In spite of her disabilities, Mary now lives an incredibly full life. She walks slowly with a cane. She goes out to lunch and to dinner with family or friends. She attends the symphony, some Board meetings, and parties; plays duplicate bridge (this is inexplicable!), and travels by car, plane, or ship as far away as London. She is always well-dressed and enjoys looking good with carefully self-selected colors and jewelry. She has her hair and nails done once a week as always. In all her activities she is as gracious and friendly as ever. She is enthusiastic and she communicates. She can ask questions and express her opinions. She can convey her feelings and tell stories. She does all this with her six words, "Hi . . bye . . no . . yes . . Oh boy." She uses some vocalizing syllables plus her increasing capacity for gesturing. It takes a great deal of patience on her part and ours. But we manage. And when we meet an impasse, we laugh, try again, or go on to something else.

"How does Mary do all this?" everyone asks. "Because she demands it," is my answer. She has always been a demanding person and still is. From the careful attention to her hair, her nails, and her proper dress, to the care of her neat and polished home; to the protection of family finances, to the meticulous and dedicated involvement with many civic activities, to the drive for educational opportunities and excellence for her three children, she has always demanded of herself and others the most and best possible. I remember once driving in a car with Mary while she drilled her young son on the vocabulary words she thought he should know. With insistent persistence, she asked for meanings: "obfuscate . . . incredulous . . . allegorical."

I am made painfully aware of the incredible demands my sister puts on herself when I am confronted with the truth of her deficits. She is able to convince others that she is more aware than she really is. But as I watch her working with her computer reading program, I am forced to understand that there are still large gaps in her language skills. She cannot readily answer simple questions. The computer asks "Where is the book?" Answers include (1) The book is red. (2) The book is on the table. (3) The book is funny. My sister looks confused, struggles, hesitantly picks out an answer. My heart hurts when I think of her prior quickness, her joy in education, her book collection. There are the times when I tell her how lovely her earrings are, she smiles appreciatively, and I ask her how she likes mine, only to get a blank look. I then realize, painfully, that she does not really understand all the spoken words that we assume she does. This time she doesn't recognize the word "mine," or possibly she didn't know it was her earrings I liked, only that I was saying something nice to her.

Mary exists on cues. With her intelligence and social skills she can observe facial expressions, intonation, and gestures to understand language even when she picks up only a noun here and there. This is similar to how I talk with a person who speaks Spanish to me. I know a few words. I know the context, and I watch the speaker. But I would find it very frustrating to live in a place where my language facility was that limited.

In fact, I have said from the very beginning that if this stroke had happened to me, I would "hide in a dark closet forever." My greatest fear in life, beyond being deaf or blind, would be to not be able to talk. Seeing my sister like this has been in a sense like seeing my greatest fear in living color. Perhaps that is why I was initially preoccupied with her. Perhaps that is why I do, at times, get so frustrated with her. Not that her demands don't get to everyone at one time or another. For example, she insists on having a shower every night, even at midnight, after the symphony and a late dinner. Someone else, usually her husband Peter, occasionally I, must undress her, put her clothes away just so, wash her, dry her, and put up her hair in rollers. This bedtime ritual may take an hour. Occasionally my impatience erupts in irritability, followed by guilt.

In the early months I was not only preoccupied, I was obsessed with thoughts of Mary and flooded with feelings of grief and anxiety. This state would lead at times to a form of depersonalization or blurring of my boundaries. I over-identified with my sister to the point that I would sometimes feel as though my gestures, my expressions, my intentions were hers. I would catch myself going by a mirror, seeing her face instead of mine. Or I would hear myself saying, "Oh boy," and feel confused as to whether she was mimicking me, or I her. I would use my right arm to brush my hair and be surprised that it worked. These were not delusional states, but something on that continuum. I had a boundary problem. I know I felt both guilt and relief that she had that terrible stroke, not I. Even today when I drive her to a restaurant, let her off near the door, then park the car and walk swiftly back, I am aware of a sense of pride and joy that I can walk freely and fast. This is accompanied by some guilt, but also gratitude and humility that I am not the one disabled.

This brings me to the second answer to "How does Mary do it?" She is able to carry on with her life because her husband Peter is an exceptionally devoted and capable caretaker. He takes care of all her personal needs, as well as taking charge of the housework and yard maintenance. Fortunately, he was retired when the stroke occurred. Handily, he has always been a very home-oriented and energetic person. He even managed to take care of everything before and after his hip replacement surgery only five months after Mary's stroke. Peter says simply "whatever is mine I take care of." I have helped, and my younger sister has helped, but Peter has the patience and dedication of Job. He gets frustrated and tired at times, but has developed through 41 years of marriage a complementary role to Mary's demanding personality. On rare occasions they each have turned to me for brief counsel, or respite, since I am the "family shrink," but mostly they prefer to be self-sufficient.

Just one year before her stroke, Peter survived two major surgeries. Mary and I spent a lot of time together then, as relatives do in a crisis. We enjoyed reminiscing and achieved an increased understanding and intimacy. It felt good. I never realized that this was to be our last chance for such sharing of memories. Now, since the stroke, our relationship has changed and deepened. We see each other much more often now, but I miss the old Mary, the verbal Mary. I'd like to know her opinions on things, her thoughts, and her feelings. There is a lot that I'll never know. Between our lunches and our laughter I feel sad.

ADDENDUM

This stroke happened to a person with many assets, financial, social, and personal. But this story is not about money, social status, or luck. It is about the occurrence of a particular kind of stroke in one particular person. Of course a change in any one of many variables would make a different story. With less fortunate circumstances psychotherapy might be indicated and useful. The major variables which may make a difference in recovery from stroke or any major illness include not only financial resources, but also the patient's support network and prior personality. In a case history such as this one, statistics and comparisons are not included. Also therapeutic suggestions would be out of place, although implicitly present. However, I believe that a psychotherapist might help by acknowledging the losses while maintaining hope; augmenting and encouraging the support systems already available; and by understanding and reinforcing the patient's previous personality style, especially as it pertains to effective ways of managing change.

Lastly, and of primary importance for the maintenance of self-esteem, is attention to the patient's core sense of self. For healthy adaptation for both the patient and the family there needs to be a sense that 'Mary is still Mary.'

Aging Lesbians:
Bearing the Burden of Triple Shame

Charity V. Schoonmaker

SUMMARY. This article contains the personal account of an aging lesbian. The author tells about her own feelings of shame (feeling defective) as a result of the effects of society's prejudice against women, lesbians, and the old. She illustrates this with examples from her life of how our culture's hidden and unconscious messages of unworthiness promote feelings of shame for the subjects of such discrimination. The particular prejudices examined are sexism, homophobia, and ageism. The author's background as a physician, first in internal medicine and later as a psychiatrist, gives a special perspective.

INTRODUCTION

My purpose in writing this article is to add the aging lesbian story to the consideration of the diverse life situations in which aging women find themselves. As we grow older, we become more different than alike inasmuch as our life experiences differ so widely.

Because of the current climate of homophobia in the small town where I practice, I am writing this article under a pseudonym. To do otherwise would mean that I would not feel safe enough to tell my personal story for fear of reprisal. I want to tell my story to illustrate what it is like to be an aging lesbian in this society today. What I feel today is the result of what my yesterdays were like. I will share

Charity V. Schoonmaker, MD, is a 64-year old psychiatrist in private practice in a small town. She is a lifelong lesbian but dares not admit this publicly. Her special interests are codependency, addictions, and working with those who come from shame-based dysfunctional families.

them so that other therapists can see what it is like for at least one aging lesbian who is coping with lifelong invisibility and who is struggling to maintain a sense of self-worth in a world which devalues women, punishes lesbians, and debases the aged.

In this article I have used the word shame to mean the feeling of being unworthy, bad, defective, unlovable, humiliated, or a mistake of creation. Shame is an overpowering human emotion and is so painful that it is frequently hidden from the self. This, perhaps, explains why shame has received so little attention in the professional literature until recently. Damaging feelings of shame are frequently on an unconscious level but still play a commanding role in influencing human behavior. We avoid, at all costs, situations which evoke our agonizing feelings of shame. Shame must be differentiated from guilt. Guilt is a feeling related to an act which violates one's values. It can be forgiven by others; whereas shame relates to one's very being and the feeling about one's self. It is not possible to forgive oneself for not being "OK."

SEXISM

I have gradually come to see how I, and lesbians of my generation, have become repositories of the systemic shame in our society. To start with, we were born female in a society which has seen females as less valuable than males. The economic advantage of this situation for the dominant males did not occur to us as we grew up despite the fact that this has been the case for thousands of years. The next shame we are heir to is that, as lesbians, we love women. This is clearly a threat to the male-dominated society because we are seen as hating men since they are not our primary love objects. It is essential for the maintenance of the male-dominated society that women nurture, love, and obey their masters. Lesbians who are not willing to do this become the objects of hate. Homophobia is the second shame; this, too, has deep roots. We almost instinctively know as young children that homosexuality is not tolerated by our society. The third shame is that of being old in a society that values youth and denies the reality of death. Further, it particularly looks down upon old women because they are valueless to men in that

they are no longer attractive sexual partners and are no longer able
to bear and rear children..

The above statements introduce what I want to discuss in human
terms–in terms of those of us who have lived with the shame of
being "less than" for our whole lives. I want to tell what it feels like
to be treated as though I were defective. At this time of my life I
know that I am not defective, but for most of my life I believed that
I truly was not "OK." The pain of living with this belief has often
been so great that I have had to hide it even from myself. Now that
I understand the sources of my pain, I want to share what that was
like, in hopes that others will understand and develop compassion
for aging lesbians, and for all other women who are not white,
Protestant, Anglo-Saxon, and heterosexual.

Now I will tell my story; knowing that it will appear in print
gives me anxiety. Even the protection of writing under a pseudonym doesn't entirely assuage my fears of being locally identified
as a lesbian in this small conservative community where it is com-
monplace to see references in our local newspaper to the moral
depravity of homosexuals. When the formation of a lesbian support
group was openly attempted, vandalism and obscene phone calls
resulted for those who were involved.

I learned at an early age that in my family being a girl clearly
meant I was a second-class citizen and there was nothing I could do
about it–I was unalterably flawed. I desperately wanted to be a boy
in order to escape that flaw; in my early childhood daydreams I was
always a boy. Later, I saw that my younger brother was seen to be
more important by my parents because he was a boy. My shame
became acute when I was told that I had "some nerve" wanting an
education because my brother's education was more important. I
was told that I should be a nurse, instead of realizing my dream of
becoming a physician. It hurt that my being an honor student didn't
make any difference; he was more entitled to an education because
he was male. Though I ultimately got a college education and a
medical education, they came through scholarships and the emotional and financial support of my grandmother, while my brother
was educated by my parents. I shall never forget my pain at being
treated as "less than" by the ones who were "supposed" to value
us equally. I could accept the unfairness of the sexism better from

the outside world than I could accept it from my parents. My mother fully accepted that she was inferior and needed a man to take care of her, since she felt she couldn't do it herself.

My college years were pivotal for me. I went to a small women's college where being career-minded was at least tolerated although not encouraged. In 1950 it was expected that we would all marry and subjugate thoughts of our own careers to those of our husbands. The alumnae news has always been blatantly heterosexist and filled only with the doings of the husbands and the children of my former classmates.

I was accepted into medical school just as the G.I.s were returning to school. I opted for a coeducational school rather than an all-women's school, reasoning that my future professional life would be with men. There were eight women in a class of two hundred, and we felt fortunate to have the support of so many women. In the other coeducational schools, there would be one or two women in a class. At that time, it was generally felt that it would be a pity to give a place to a woman in a medical school class when there were so many "deserving" men coming back from the Service wanting a medical education. Women, it was well known, marry and give up their professions.

In medical school I was in a blatantly sexist world. The women were the butt of daily jokes. Our motives for going into medicine were always questioned, since women couldn't possibly have the same reasons that men had for going through the rigors of medical school. In our course work, it was made abundantly clear that women were viewed primarily as sex objects and persons to bear and raise children. We could count on some of the slides in pathology class being of seductive women. They always got a laugh, and I always got an uncomfortable feeling in the pit of my stomach. It never crossed my mind to object or even to feel that I was being abused. I felt that in order to become a physician, I had to accept this kind of treatment or else I would have been considered weak and, therefore, unfit for the profession.

There was much more abuse, not all of it sexist. After all, one had to be "tough" to be a physician. We all lived in terror of flunking out, and the school administration fostered this fear.

When I moved into the clinical years, I learned that women

patients were only "complainers," but men were considered signif-icantly ill when they had the same symptoms of illness. Old women were especially likely to be called "crocks," and their complaints were seldom taken seriously. Under the pressures of too little sleep, too much to do in too little time, too much responsibility for our limited experience, and too much humiliation by superiors, we all learned to join the oppressors. I became critical of women and unsympathetic with women's issues. I became intolerant of feel-ings–my own or anybody else's. I had internalized the views of the sexist white male in order to separate myself from the shame of being a despised female. I look back on this period of my life with great guilt over the way I treated my patients. I did not see their emotional pain because I did not see my own. I was a product of an abusive system, and I in turn was abusive.

When it came time for internship and residency selection, the women of the class knew that women needn't bother to apply for the most coveted positions, because these were for men only. While we grumbled about this, we simply accepted the status quo.

After years of practice of internal medicine and personal therapy, I gradually came to be aware of my own feelings and those of my patients. I came to see that my patients' emotional pain was far greater than their physical pain, yet I lacked the tools to help them in the ways they needed most. After much soul searching, I went back into residency training to become a psychiatrist.

In my naivete, I imagined that 38 years later the abusive system of medical education had changed. Wrong! I found myself back in the same sexist system which humiliates patient and trainee alike. Once more I survived my residency training, but this time the price I paid for survival was depression. This time around I was very much in touch with my feelings; my suffering was intense. I saw sexual harassment of patients and staff, and I saw inhumane treat-ment of patients and staff. I felt helpless to help my patients or myself in the abusive system and hopeless about changing it. I could not feel self worth and still put up with the daily abuses and indignities. In the end, my only recourse was to change to another residency program where the abuses were considerably less. I mar-veled at the way my younger colleagues were unaware of the abuses–just as I had been in my youth.

When I look back on my 64 years of living in such a rampantly sexist society, I am amazed at how long it took me to realize how the doctrine of white male supremacy has poisoned our society, and how much shame and pain it has caused. Behind it all is economics. Men profit from the unpaid and underpaid work of women. The men must keep the power in order to enforce this system, which profits them and only them.

What I have stated so far may, indeed, sound like the man-hating of which feminists, lesbians, and old women have been so often accused. I do hate the system but not individual men. The question is whether one looks at this from a systemic and societal view or from the view of the individual. I feel that to blame individual men for the societal shame that has been placed on women is to take a very limited view of our culture. It is my belief that today's women are partially responsible for perpetuating the sexist system because they frequently raise their sons to be dominant and their daughters to accept the same inferior role that they were taught to accept. Today's men, accepting their dominant role, also are responsible for perpetuating the abusive system. Both genders suffer from living stereotypic roles, though they suffer in different ways. Perhaps men suffer more than women do, since they die earlier, and the rate of suicide amongst men rises rapidly with age. I have mostly worked with men all of my professional life; as a physician, I have taken care of a great many men. I see that the price men pay for their economic supremacy and power base is very great. This price, as I see it, is the loss of the ability to have and share feelings. To be without the ability to communicate on a feeling level means the loss of intimate relationships. This is a terrible loss. I know what it is like–I have been a woman living in a man's world unable to express my feelings and unable to experience the joy of truly intimate relationships.

My point is to address the unconscious shame (and, hopefully the conscious shame as well) that we women feel when we are labeled "not OK" simply because we are born female in our sexist system. Not to address sexism openly means that we women will forever remain its victims. My life has shown me over and over how wrong sexism is and that if it isn't challenged it will continue from generation to generation.

HOMOPHOBIA

Homophobia is the second origin of shame of which I will write. To understand what role it has played in the lives of lesbians over 60, it is necessary to look at the times. I became 18 years old at the close of World War II. It was a time when men came back from the war to reclaim their "rightful" place in society, i.e., one of dominance. A new wave of homophobia swept the nation as men sought the jobs held by women during the war, expecting the women to return to their previous subservient roles. College deans expelled students for lesbian attachments; my college was no exception. In my sophomore year I met my life partner, and my whole life changed. At first, I didn't understand my attraction for her; then I tried to believe that our relationship was not homosexual. The truth was that I had fallen in love with Doris. What joy! What pain! I was terrified of discovery; but I could not give up the happiness I found with her. I never before experienced such happiness in all my 19 years. I was terribly conflicted and confused and dared not speak of it to anyone. I felt completely alone in the world with my problem, save for Doris. When away from her I felt despairing, and my grades plummeted. Even though it is now 44 years later, I shall never forget the pain of hiding my love and feeling that being homosexual meant that I was defective and loathsome. In spite of those feelings, I found that I could not give up the most wonderful thing that had ever happened to me; my isolation began. I hid from family, friends, and co-workers. Once, in those early days, I told two old friends about my new relationship, and I never heard from either again.

Later, in medical school, I isolated myself from fellow students and was terrified that discovery of my sexual orientation would end my hopes for a medical career. If even the word homosexual was used in my presence my mouth got dry and my heart pounded. I carefully wiped out any traces of a personal life in my conversations with co-workers, and refused all social invitations. I continued to be alone with my shame.

After I went into practice, my fear of discovery became even greater, and we almost completely excluded the world outside of our relationship. We hungered for friends with whom we could be ourselves but dared not take the risk of disclosing the truth about our relationship. We became very focused on each other and hid the pain of our isolation. Outside our home I behaved as though Doris didn't exist. Ten years ago when I made the decision to leave my practice of internal medicine to enter a psychiatric residency program in a distant big city, I realized I couldn't face the rest of my life in such isolation, I decided I would seek lesbian and gay friendships and risk being more open. When I applied to the second residency program, I found, to my horror, that I was telling the director of the program about my sexual orientation. I was aghast at what I had done; but I guess I was so tired of hiding that it just slipped out! Fortunately he accepted me into the program, and the dam was broken! I gradually crawled out of the "closet," and to my great relief nobody was unable to handle my disclosure of my sexual orientation.

In that distant city I felt safe to join both a homosexual physicians' group and a lesbian social group. What a relief to be open and to include my partner! What a joy to be in a whole roomful of women who were all lesbian! I no longer felt so alone, and my feelings of defectiveness began to wane. When I prepared to talk on psychiatry and homosexuality for a homosexual physicians' group, I came to see that not all of psychiatry saw us as mentally ill. While I had learned that homosexuality wasn't immoral or sinful, I still had believed that I was "sick." Therapy had not dispelled this belief, since it was with a psychiatrist who subscribed to the theories of "penis envy" (male superiority) and "arrested development" of homosexuals (sickness).

Once connected with other gays and lesbians, I no longer felt so unaccepted and alone, and I could feel my sense of shame lessening. This helped me to have the courage to "come out" to my brother and my mother, who had never acknowledged to themselves or to me that I was a lesbian. Neither of them disowned me, as I had feared they might; rather, my honesty paved the way for better relationships with both of them than I had ever had.

When it came time to return to our home city, I knew that I could never again deny my lesbian orientation to the important people in my life. I had lived in the "closet" too long. Though I have been fearful of the outcome, I now am open with colleagues in the mental-health field and with many friends. I dare not reveal my orientation to the general public or to my patients. If I did so, I fear the repercussions would be ugly in this reactionary community.

As I look back over these last ten years, I am amazed at how much my life has changed and how much my shame has receded. I would not have believed I would feel so much better about myself through "coming out." I wish I had not been so closeted for so much of my life. Yet I know that my fears about disclosing my lesbian self were real, and that they continue to be real with the current rise of homophobia in the wake of AIDS and recent economic hardship.

AGING

The third of the three shames that I have had to face is caused by ageism. After spending the first two-thirds of my life learning to deal with the internalized shame of being both a woman and a lesbian, I am very tired of being invisible and unimportant. The negative stereotypes used against the old feel just like those used against women and lesbians–hurtful, patronizing, demeaning, objectifying, dehumanizing, and cruel. I wonder what my fate will be in the hands of a society which considers everything, even its people, disposable. It is chilling for me to consider that I am reaching the age when I, too, will be trashed by society just like the used hamburger wrapper, because both of us have seemingly outlived our usefulness. It has been such a struggle for me to have the freedom to be who I am, and now I face the loss of my sense of self again. I am facing the loss of my professional identity as I retire and am no longer "important" to society as a worker. I fear there is increasing resentment on the part of the young about taking care of the old. This will grow as the numbers of us, the aged, grow larger in proportion to the population-at-large and are seen as an economic burden. I fear increasingly vicious attacks on the old. It doesn't seem to occur to the young that with luck (reaching old age), they, too, will feel the pain of ageism–being considered worthless.

On a more personal level, I fear living beyond any meaningful life. I also fear that society will deny to me my final freedom–the right to die when life has lost its savor. I fear losing my partner;

Doris has been with me for two-thirds of my life, and I cannot imagine a happy existence without her abiding love and support. I have worked with those left behind by death, and I know that life is never the same without one's partner. I am afraid of being sick and helpless, of not being in control of my life. I am afraid of being objectified–treated as a thing without a human identify–an old woman and a despised lesbian as well. I fear that medical care will be denied to me, as I see that Medicare has the effect of limiting care by administrative fiat. I fear that if I must leave my home, there will be no place for me to live and still maintain my identify as a lesbian. I don't want to have to go back to living the lie of life as a heterosexual, to have to pretend that the best part of life didn't exist! What could I safely share about my life in a senior center or in a nursing home?

I have thought a lot about ageism. I think the root of it lies in our American culture's denial of death. Like so many other forms of denial, our denial of death prevents us from dealing with the pain of knowing that it is inevitable that we die; that it is even a good thing to be mindful of the finiteness of our lives so that we live our lives today to the fullest. But death is not to be considered in polite company–notice the ensuing silence or change of subject when death is mentioned. In death we lose all that we have ever known, but that is less fearsome to me than a living death of invisibility and worthlessness.

Although ageism affects both genders, it is women who suffer most. Old men are valued much more. Old women aren't only devalued; they are feared when they are no longer seen to be under the sexual domination of men. Considering the well-known fact that old women greatly outnumber old men, I look forward to the day when old women take back their power from the men and the unthinking young. I also feel called upon to help this process when I can't be hurt professionally by the inevitable backlash. I believe that only old women can have the insight and the intestinal fortitude to change our society to one where people are more important than things, and each person is treated with respect and humaneness.

CONCLUSION

I have spoken of my life in this article in a way I have never done before. Although I have experienced some fear about doing so, I hope my story may touch you so that you may touch others. I would like to add that in spite of my lifelong battle to feel "OK" about myself in the face of our sexist, homophobic, and ageist culture, I am happier today than I ever was in the past. I also feel that dealing with my pain has helped me be more authentic in my life and has made me able to be more in touch with the pain of others. The worst thing I can do for me or for others at this time in my life is to be silent when so much needs saying, both for me and the millions of other aging lesbians in America.

I think that the implications for therapists dealing with aging lesbians are first, to be aware of the diversity of aging women's life experience and not assume heterosexuality or asexuality. Second, a therapist should be aware of the depths of shame a client may feel regarding any lesbian experience, and that shame prevents her from talking about what most needs to be brought out in the therapeutic process. Third, a therapist (especially if younger) needs to be very sensitive regarding the issues of unconscious ageism, homophobia, and sexism, both in client and the therapist. Adequate supervision is a necessity for the therapist who has not yet worked through these issues. Living in this society, none of us can claim having escaped these biases. Fourth, homosexuality is not a mental illness but does complicate making a healthy adjustment to life's problems and tragedies.

Three Native American Women Speak About the Significance of Ceremony

Aleticia Tijerina-Jim

SUMMARY. In greater numbers, Native health care givers are caring for Native American people. This article explores the significance of ceremony from the perspective of three Native women elders. Choctaw shop proprietor Phyllis Hogan explains how she was able to accept her aging when at 40 years old she performed a menstruation ceremony. Lorena Lomatuwayma is head of the sacred Mazua (Women's Society) in Hotevilla, Arizona. She reflects upon the spiritual significance of ceremony in a Hopi's life. Medicine Woman Mary K. Boone is a well-known Navajo herbalist and healer. She describes her role as elder and advisor in her culture and speaks about the Navajo view of death.

Her small, pueblo-style shop in downtown Flagstaff, Arizona is brightly colored. Turquoise Hopi sun-faces border stone; here and there a yellow painted lizard crawls toward the sky. Others have complained, but when the shop owner's daughter painted the Spanish iron bars across the windows blue, she and her mom decided the look was unique. Other things are different about the shop too: a coyote mask; superbly crafted jewelry by Native American artists; scattered stones and red pots with herbs carefully placed on a woven grey rug; and the shop owner, herself. The shop owner is unique.

The Winter Sun Trading Company is owned by a part Choctaw, part Irish woman who has spent more than half of her life studying native herbs and the native people who use them. Phyllis Hogan is a

Aleticia Tijerina-Jim is a Chicana "new" writer. She is a poet and writes on political and spiritual issues. She is presently working on a collection of short stories about Native American lives. She lives in Flagstaff, AZ with her family.

33

doctor: a tall, sturdy-boned woman whose waist-length sandy brown hair and quick wit have made her famous. She is vibrant and sexy and has a tainted reputation for being bold and outspoken, very much her "own woman."

"Women can never really accept themselves until they accept their femaleness–which of course means accepting their blood from menstruation," Phyllis told me matter-of-factly.

"When I turned 40, I suddenly realized I was not connected to my body. So I went back–to connect with my femaleness. I took rags that I had made out of diapers and let myself bleed into them. Then I ritualistically rinsed my bloody rags in a wicker basket and poured my blood into the ground. I prayed, saying, 'I give back this blood to my mother.'"

"Honoring the earth with my own blood was my own personal way to initiate myself into eldership," she said.

Initiation into femaleness is an old concept for Native women. Ceremonies at the time of birth and puberty are the most common. However, Hopi elder Lorena Lomatuwayma said there is another ceremony that will carry a woman to the spirit world.

Lorena moves slowly around her Flagstaff apartment. She is the middle child from a family of twelve boys and four girls. She was told by her father that he had asked for her in a ceremony called the Grinding Girls. She is from the Corn Clan. She was reared in Hotevilla, Arizona and is Head of the religious Maxua Women's Society.

At 59, Lorena's soft, short, thick hair bobs around her gentle face and gives her the appearance of a young school girl. Her black eyes slant in two different directions, and she seldom seems to be looking at you. As a child, Lorena's teachers had considered her retarded and had ignored her; Lorena became too embarrassed to ask her teachers what was written on the chalk board. But the truth was, Lorena is legally blind–not stupid. She dropped out of school early, married, and bore eight children before divorcing her husband and moving to Flagstaff. She was 49 before she could challenge her handicap. One day, her eldest daughter sent a professor to her home. He asked her to participate in a reading program at Northern Arizona University. At first she hesitated, but her children convinced her to participate. Two weeks later Lorena could read braille. Presently, she is helping Professor Ekkehart Malotki to translate the first Hopi dictionary. Lorena's wisdom is evident in her words to me.

"Initiation to the Kachinas is the most important ceremony left to our people," Lorena said. "Today, many Hopis are not initiated and cannot participate in our ceremonies."

Lorena explained that Kachinas are spirit beings who instruct and guide the people in their everyday lives. Because the Kachinas represent Hopi lives, new Kachinas such as "the gambler" have been added to the older, less fanciful ones. However, Lorena believes the children should be learning from the older ones. Lorena was also adamant that the young should be joining the religious societies.

"I want to encourage our young to initiate into the Woman's Society or the Man's Society because it is our religion. They say once you learn to participate in the Women's Society that is how you learn to pray to God. Our God, Mawsaw, who is the One who lived here when we came to Old Oraibi, said to the people, 'I am not going to give you this land because you are not going to repent.' Mawsaw said the people had crazy things on their minds. He told us he would give us the kivas and our societies so we can learn to pray and to give back to him what we owe him.

"We owe Mawsaw for this land. It is like we are renters and He is the landlord. Our societies teach us how to pay him back."

Many traditionally-based Native societies either formally or in an informal agreement chose leaders such as Lorena to head The Society and make spiritual decisions. Because Native American ceremonies are centered around a deep, profound awe of the natural—sun, stone, moon—and ceremonies are conducted in such a way as to honor all living things as brothers and sisters, a natural equality is born. Within these religious contexts, women are equal and have recognized, sometimes clearly defined powers.

A difference which sets Native cultures apart from non-Native cultures is the marking of time. Both Navajos and Hopis mark significant human development into four stages. Birth marks the first of these. For example, Hopis observe a 20-day ceremony starting at birth until the 20th day when the baby is named and "given over" to the community. Both Navajos and Hopis conduct puberty rites which Lorena said are called "taking the rough way." Special rites are observed during the time a woman is in her child-bearing years. A woman's menses are considered holy, and if the woman observes the special rites and taboos during the time of her menstruation then the people say she will lead a happy, balanced life.

Growing old is the fourth stage. Like the other three stages, this fourth stage of life gives a person special powers. Hopi elder women are expected to bear more responsibilities within the villages, such as caring for and preparing for the Kachinas. Navajo elder women become "stateswomen" who make decisions about land and children.

Respect for the old is a strong value within both the Navajo and Hopi cultures. Growing old does not have the same stigma attached to it as within other cultures. This is evident by the complex language cues that are used by the Navajos. How you address people, what title you give them, will reveal the relationship you are expected to have between yourselves. For example, if I were to meet an older woman whom I am told is the same clan as my mother, then I would address her as Shimasani, my maternal grandmother. In turn, I would be expected to treat her like my mother, giving her respect and care, and asking her for advice. Extended family networks will care for the old, but changes are occurring.

Mary K. Boone is a beautiful 60 year-old Navajo elder with bright black eyes and a few silver streaks highlighting her long black hair. Her smile is electric. The day I met her wrists were adorned with old-style squash blossom turquoise and silver bracelets, and she was wearing a long flowing maroon "Navajo" skirt.

I had heard many stories about Mary. She is considered a powerful medicine woman, having spent her entire life learning about native herbs and then using them to cure. Her late husband, Sam Boone, Sr., was a medicine man as well. Her other powers came from his use of peyote within the Native American Church. Sam had been a "Road Man," a position within the NAC comparable to a priest.

When I met Mary, I was surprised to hear her complain about the young. Her arguments sounded familiar. "The youth today want too many things."

"When my kids were growing up they never asked me for anything. Now, I have 13 grandkids, and my daughter's oldest son wants a new truck for his graduation," Mary said.

I asked her what she thought was the cause of this new, yet surprising generational gap.

"I think our children are losing their language in the schools, and this is the cause. Parents today are not making their children learn the old ways. Parents today are not making their children learn Navajo language. Medicine people should be allowed in the schools to teach. This would help the people stay strong."

I was reminded of an incident some years back on the Northern Arizona University campus. One spring, lightning struck the newly built Natatorium. Navajo students refused to go there unless they could bring in a medicine man to conduct a ceremony which would repair the spiritual damage caused by the lightning. Navajos believe that any object struck by lightning is a sign of a spiritual imbalance. Ceremonies to restore this balance are central to Navajo religious belief and practice. But how much more damage is being done unknowingly to a traditional people who must study and work in environments which are considered spiritually imbalanced, and which will cause illness and death?

Death is a topic which is sensitive to everyone. Navajo traditional taboos make it impossible for someone to speak the name of a dead relative. Homes where someone has died are traditionally abandoned. However, these rules are being relaxed. Mary agreed to speak a little about the death of her husband and how Navajos view death. She said she hopes this knowledge will help others when dealing with Navajos in institutions. She also asked that you remember to ask your Native clients if they need a medicine man or woman.

"Sam knew he was going to die. He was not really sick, but he knew he was going to die. One day he told me, I am going to die, so don't cry for me," Mary said.

Native American views about death and the afterlife may be the biggest factor separating Native thought from the Euro-Christian view. Neither traditional Hopis nor Navajos believe in a heaven or hell. Hopis believe you will return to the traditional home of the Kachinas in the San Francisco Peaks or the Grand Canyon. Navajos believe that, when you die, where your spirit goes will depend on how you "thought" in your lifetime. The key factor to a happy afterlife is a balanced life. Navajo ceremonies are conducted to help a person restore this balance–thus achieving happiness in the here-after.

"We Navajos don't believe in a heaven or hell. This is a Christian way of thinking. We believe there is no death. We tell our children we will always be with them. We believe every living thing has a spirit, and we are all made of spirit.

"People today don't tell their kids about death. We Navajos, well, the older ones, we tell our kids about death. We tell them we will always be with them, so don't be crying for me.

"This way of thinking makes us strong," Mary said.

"Yes it does," I said.

CONCLUSION

Both Mary and Lorena strongly believe that Native American medicine healers, chanters, singers, or Holy women and men should be allowed to assist physicians when caring for Native patients in hospitals, nursing homes, treatment centers, or at home. At the request of the patient, a medicine woman or man could be brought into the hospital or treatment center to conduct a healing ceremony. I have witnessed a few events of this kind, and the results were very positive. When problems did arise, it was because an uninformed staff had become unnecessarily concerned about smoke (herbs are burned during ceremonies) and noise. If the support staff is well-informed about what will occur, these problems can be avoided. Recently, the American Cancer Society conducted a seminar introducing Native medicine healers to an audience of interested health professionals. Native American medicine healers were able to share their knowledge in a forum designed to give respect and homage to their way of healing. What resulted, I am sure, was a small group of doctors, nurses, and counselors more culturally aware and more sensitive to the spiritual needs of their Native American patients.

Another factor in delivering culturally-sensitive care to Native American patients is to allow the patient to attend a Native "church" service (Native American Church). These ceremonies often require elaborate preparation and can last for several days.

Physicians and families might arrange for partial attendance by the patient, or perhaps agree to an alternative service in the hospital or treatment center. Medication during a ceremony will continue to be a complex issue. However, the Arizona Ethnobotanical Research Association in Flagstaff, founded by Phyllis Hogan, conducts research on the medicinal properties of native herbs. Physicians could readily match these findings against their modern pharmaceutical counterparts and balance a combination of native herbs and drugs as a solution to caring for Native American patients.

One must understand that Native Americans are truly caught between two worlds–their own, ordered universe of song, dance, ritual, language, and thought, oftentimes pitted against a foreign world which is threatening to devour them. Before it was simple: a crushed bird egg was the cause of the "burning" illness, or cancer. Now, the questions are not so simple. And neither can be the answers.

Confronting Ageism:
A MUST for Mental Health

Shevy Healey

SUMMARY. This is a personal account by a 70 year old lesbian of how she came to the conclusion that without confronting ageism it is impossible to have a good old age.

The equation of old women with undesirability is so pervasive that no one is immune from its destructiveness. The fear about age, reaching phobic proportions among white skinned women of European background, has grave repercussions for us as we experience our own aging. We can attempt to deny our aging for a while at least, through the almost universal practice of trying to pass for younger; we can accept the ugly stereotypes about ourselves and become increasingly depressed and alienated; or we can embark on the struggle to confront the ageism of our culture as well as our own internalized ageism.

As an old woman who has chosen the latter course, the impact upon my life has been tremendous. In this article I speak of my struggles against my own internalized ageism and how this path led me to a renewed social activism, sense of purpose, and inner exploration. I have been forced to explore the actuality of my aging vs. my ageist expectations, which I have found repeatedly to cloud my ability to experience my life. This process has brought excitement and fullness to my life, making my old age a time rich in learning and insight.

Old age crept upon me and caught me unawares.
Like most women, I had never thought about my own growing

Shevy Healey is a retired 70 year old psychotherapist with a PhD in Clinical Psychology from The Ohio State University. Formerly in private practice, she is a feminist actively involved as a writer, presenter, and facilitator, as well as one of the founders of the Old Lesbians Organizing for Change (OLOC), a national organization by and for old lesbians 60 and over dedicated to confronting ageism.

41

old. When I was young I felt invincible. In my 30's I was too busy struggling through my life to think about any future. I do remember thinking longingly of "retirement" but that was because I didn't like my life very much and felt powerless to change it.

In my 40's and 50's, with my life exploding in many new directions, I felt, in my heart of hearts, that I was beating the clock. I first began my college education at age 43 and not too long thereafter got divorced after some 22 years of marriage. I continued and finished my undergraduate work while my only child was herself away at college. Deciding to go for broke, at 47 I left Southern California where I had lived most of my adult life to go to graduate school in Ohio, and at 54 I finally got a Ph.D. in clinical psychology. At 50 I made another drastic life change when I fell in love with a woman and came out as a lesbian.

With so much going on for me, I did not feel in sync with my peers and fooled myself into thinking, when I thought of age at all, that it was "a state of mind," nothing else. The experience of being out of sync was, in fact, what felt most familiar.

My mother, father, and I arrived in this country from Poland in 1923. Within six months my father died, and at age 24 my mother was left alone without any close family to raise a two year old child. I started kindergarten not knowing a word of English, and my sense of shame and alienation was more profound when my first name was arbitrarily changed by the school registrar. My own name was too "foreign" sounding; thus Sheva became Evelyn.

Although almost all immigrants were poor, we were in an especially impoverished category. At the height of the Great Depression when my mother got sick and could no longer bring home even the four dollars a week she was earning we were forced to go on county welfare to survive.

I was out of sync even as a Jewish child raised in a Jewish ghetto, for my mother was a revolutionary and an atheist. I was the only child I knew who ate bread on Pessach (Passover), and who "on principle" did not say aloud the Pledge of Allegiance to a government which hypocritically claimed to be for liberty and justice for all, while favoring the rich at the expense of the poor. At five I proudly marched with my mother, a garment worker, on my first picket line. I clearly remember running with her down an alley to escape the Philadelphia mounted police, who, with horses rearing and stomping, charged into the picket line of mostly women and children in an attempt to break the strike. By age eleven I was a seasoned Junior Pioneer leader wearing my red bandanna and marching in picket lines and May Day Parades. From the rebellious tom boy to the high school rebel, I was an "expert" in knowing what it felt like to be other than the mainstream, while at the same time having a strong sense of place and solidarity with my own political comrades.

The closest I came to being mainstream was when I finally got my Ph.D., but by then I was an "out" lesbian and feminist–both of which did not exactly clothe me in respectability.

Surely then, with all of my previous experience of otherness, I could be expected to make a relatively easy transition to the otherness experienced so acutely by old women. Absolutely not so. I continued through my 50's steadfast in my delusion that age, *my* age, was irrelevant. More and more in social circles I experienced myself as the "older" woman in the group, but coming out as a lesbian at 50 and having a wonderfully exciting decade only promoted my sense of myself as an exception. It is true that I began to fret about my outward appearance more than I ever had. The wrinkles, loose flesh, the changes in my body left me worried and split. How could my body feel so charged and sexual, my self be so full of plans and dreams and energy, while at the same time it was registering the signs of growing old? Although I never dyed my hair, by now a lovely steel gray, I did seriously consider a face lift. Only at the last minute did I acknowledge to myself that it would take more than surgery to help me resolve my internal split about my own aging.

My growing external change of status forced my growing internal discomfort to reach more conscious levels. My first intimations of what age stereotyping was all about occurred when I moved into a new community and was shocked to find myself addressed by younger people, with the ritual respect reserved for–not Mother–but Grandmother, at a time when my own grandchild had not yet been born. I began to work only part time and this meant increasing isolation from colleagues and work–related sources of respect. I found also that younger professionals who were meeting me for the

first time and knew that I too was a professional assumed a respect-
ful rather than collegial stance, while those who knew nothing
about me most often ignored me completely.

My own mother and step-father, now in their early 80's, seemed
to be having increasing health difficulties, but I must admit, strange
as that seems to me now, I simply did not pay much attention and
blithely assumed that they would go on as always, at least until
some far-off future. My world changed radically and shockingly
when my step-father died unexpectedly after surgery, leaving my
mother alone, in failing health and total panic. Suddenly I found
myself solely and increasingly responsible for my mother's care, a
task which took enormous energy and struggle.

When she died some two years later at age 85, no amount of
preparation helped me to experience my new position in the world,
feeling orphaned at 63! I became the oldest living member of my
very small family. In a way I could not foresee I was catapulted into
an active awareness of my own mortality, my own vulnerability,
myself as an old woman.

There ensued a series of struggles and learnings which I think are
relatively typical, though at the time I thought were unique. The
invisibility I experienced as an old woman felt much different from
all the experiences of otherness I had ever known. Being subject to
special oppression was certainly familiar enough. What was different this time, however, was how I felt inside as I experienced this
oppression. Whatever fear I had experienced in being "other"
throughout my life, I had always felt a core of strength and pride in
who I was and what I stood for–in my poor and working class
background, my Jewishness, my atheism, my foreignness, my political radicalism, my being a girl, a woman, a lesbian. Now, I was
attempting to deny my otherness by denying my own aging, a
denial that masked the tremendous fear I felt about being an old
woman, about being "over the hill," for I had internalized the ageist
stereotype that my life was all but over and I did not want it to be!
Neither did I want to be part of a group stigmatized as ineffectual,
useless, ugly, asexual, whining, passive, lifeless, sick, dependent,
powerless–the antithesis of everything I had tried to be and make of
my life.

What a dilemma: hating and dreading what being old represented, while each year becoming more clearly identifiably old. All I really wanted was to hold back the clock by some magical act of will. Truth is, I think I tried that–for a while convincing myself that if only I exercised the right way, ate the right food, lived the right kind of pure and glowing life, I would "beat" old age. I never, as yet, questioned the validity of my ageist assumptions. My fears were reinforced by watching my mother grow old and die, an old age that was full of denial and fear of the changes occurring in her body and her life, and rage at what she considered the whittling away of her self and the ending of a life that felt unfulfilled.

Looking back on that time, only now can I see how hard I was working to deny my feelings and my confusion. It was, of course, not possible to deal with a problem that I refused to identify, for I was doing what all oppressed groups try to do; I was trying to pass–to myself at least. Knowing that I felt inside a continuity with the person I always was, instead of realizing that growing old does not mean dropping off a precipice, I decided I felt "young" inside. But no matter how automatic and unconscious this universal practice of passing for younger is, it remains a deeply alienating experience. Begging the question, refusing to acknowledge my age did nothing but rob me of the core of strength I needed to sustain and guide me through this great life change, crossing the bridge between mid-life and old.

Finally, the reality of my life forced me to go beyond denial and into acknowledging and coping somehow with my unaccustomed and unwanted status of being an old woman. In the beginning of this struggle I found myself wavering between rage–at the patronizing dismissals meted out to me in many different forms, and anxiety and foreboding about my future.

Having just turned 70, I can look at my last decade and chart my progress to a rich and rewarding old age. I am able to view my own process within the context of the political, not simply the personal. This pushes me to share my experience in the hope that it can be useful to other women learning to grow up to be old. But although I think the issue has universal significance, denial about the process is so ingrained that it seems somewhat daring, even brave, to speak in detail about my own struggles to explore the dimensions of being an old woman. For the most part, neither books nor songs are written about the every day, heroic and ordinary lives of old women. Talk about being old by the old is a conversational taboo. Interestingly, only young and mid-life women feel free to speak easily and insultingly of their dread of coming into my time of life.

I owe a huge debt to Barbara Macdonald and the book she wrote with Cynthia Rich, *Look Me In The Eye–Old Women Aging and Ageism* (1991). When I read and reread this book I felt a profound and exhilarating relief. For in writing about her own life Macdonald had also named my experience and made me feel sane, less alone and less fearful. It reminds me of the excitement of discovery we women experienced in the early days of the women's movement when we learned through our consciousness raising groups as nothing else could teach us, that what was happening in our lives was not a matter of individual flaw or problem but a common experience of oppression.

So, too, has this time of my life been a sorting, testing, learning, both as I become more mindful and attentive to my own experience and as I share with other old women and learn from our common experience. Yet this ongoing process is complex and I often feel muddled and overwhelmed. When that happens, I long to find some systematic simple way, because I am that kind of a person, to categorize and define the various components of my experience.

Am I dealing, in any given instance, with the ageism, sexism, heterosexism, or anti-semitism of our society? Am I being "too" sensitive? Certainly as an old Jewish lesbian I can expect to and mostly do get treated in certain predictable ways in our oppressive mainstream culture, but my dismay is more acute when I experience the same slights, the same invisibility in my own special lesbian and feminist community. Since old women, lesbian or heterosexual, are invisible in our society, it is easy to grow used to that condition and sometimes the only clue I have that I am in the world but not part of it is an uneasy delayed reaction I have to my own invisibility. It is not always clear at first.

Or am I dealing not just with external ageism but a response that arises from my own internalized ageism, buttressed by the sexist and heterosexist models of aging I have from my mother and her generation?

Or, finally, can I trust that my response is actually coming from inside me, from my own body of life experience?

Sometimes there seems almost no area of behavior and emotion in which I can totally trust my first reaction. In almost every part of my life I am forced again and again to examine my ageist expectations, not because I necessarily want to do so from some intellectual curiosity, but because if I do not do this, false expectations and assumptions cloud and diminish my ability to actually experience my life.

I think often of the most important model I've had–my own mother and her unfulfilled old age. I have to remind myself that her life and my life have been vastly different, that the times in which we both lived, the options we had and choices we made were vastly different. I remind myself also of the research that points out that in old age there is greater heterogeneity than at any other developmental stage, which provides even less basis for the existing stereotypes about old women. Yet these cultural assumptions harden into oppressive dogmas. Ageism, primarily a woman's issue, is the extension of the sexism, heterosexism, racism, and rampant consumerism of our multi-corporate society. Old women, outliving men in greater numbers, have lost their special capacity for service to the patriarchy. They no longer function as ornaments, lovers, domestics, bearers and rearers of children, or as economic drudges in the work place. To quote Copper (1988), "The ageism which old women experience is firmly embedded in sexism, an extension of the male power to define, control values, erase, disempower and divide."

The expressions of ageism are many. A core area of my ongoing examination of my own aging is my self and my relationship to my body. This is a most complex relationship, encompassing issues of illness and wellness, fear of incapacity and actual disability, loss of independence and acceptance of interdependence, the intricate relationship of my body and appearance to my sense of self and self-esteem, my own standards and politics of beauty, and more. The interrelationship and the complexity of all of these issues make them difficult to untangle. I find comfort in reminding myself that I am not dealing with trivialities but with the core issues that we all face throughout our entire lives. The fear of aging, reaching phobic proportions among white skinned women of European background, has grave repercussions for women as they experience their own aging. My greater urgency to confront these issues is my conviction that my health, well being and life itself rest on finding my way through the swamp of the ageist myths and assumptions.

My appearance was the first indicator I could see of my own aging. The face lift that I didn't get compelled me instead to examine my assumptions about beauty and appearance. It forced me to begin specifically to confront the basic assumption underlying ageism, that youth is good, desirable, and beautiful; old age is bad, repulsive and ugly. Otherwise every time I look in the mirror I must feel contempt and aversion for how I look, or avoid looking altogether because, by patriarchal standards of beauty, I will find no beauty there.The most frequent "compliment" given to old women is "you don't look your age." Consider for a moment that what is really being said is that if you did look your age you would look ugly. There is an erosion of the self which occurs when who you are is everywhere made synonymous with unattractiveness and undesirability.

I was thrilled to read Cynthia Rich's article on Ageism and the Politics of Beauty (1988), which challenges us to look at how we arrive at our ideas about beauty and to reconsider the "mysteries of attraction." For unless we examine these "mysteries" we may well exclude, to our impoverishment, whole categories of women as attractive, particularly those who are disabled or old. Rich says, "Our task is to learn, not to look insultingly beyond these features to a soul we can celebrate, but instead to take at these bodies as parts of these souls–exciting, individual, beautiful."

My first big stretch then was to examine my own conditioned notions and reconsider more open ways to experience beauty. Most helpful to me in this process is the greater reliance I have been developing on my own senses, rather on preconceived ideas. Skin that is old and wrinkled is soft and lovely, and as I touch my own skin and that of my lover I feel deep pleasure. Letting go more and more of my conditioning makes it possible for me to look with a clearer more loving vision at myself and the other old women around me. A shift, not yet complete, is taking place.

My relationship to my body has always been somewhat problematic. I have lived much of my life in my head and was trained, even more so than most women, to ignore my body's demands either for rest or attention. With growing psychological sophistication I talked about and regularly included in my practice as a therapist the notion of making friends with one's body. However, outside of sporadic frenzied efforts, I myself continued largely to ignore my body, and seemed to be able to do so with impunity since for the most part I was blessed with good health.

But starting in my 60's, my body no longer permits me to ignore her; she has begun to speak most loudly on her own behalf. Although I've always eaten too quickly and too much, for the first time I began to develop digestive problems. My vision, even with glasses, has become strained, and I've had laser surgery for glaucoma in both eyes. I have found that it takes me longer to recuperate, either after hard work or a transient illness, and I get downright cranky with insufficient rest. In other words, my body is showing some wear and tear after a long and arduous life. Certainly an acceptable proposition in a sane society and one that can be lived with, particularly since so many of us have paid such lip service to the need for women to attend to ourselves and our bodies with kindness and care, not only to others.

But in our culture, one of the first ageist assumptions is that to be old automatically means to be in some state of failing health and decrepitude, physical, mental, or both, and, further, to be in this state means to be valueless and a non-person. It is no wonder, then, that women from their thirties on begin to lament their failing physical abilities, as if the standard set in the teens and 20's are the normative standards for life. My experiences with health limitations were so tied in with ageist expectations that at the first signs of what turned out to be a relatively mild condition I had a life crisis. I will not ever forget the absolutely unreasoning fear I felt the night I finally called the paramedics for what I thought was probably gas, but "given my age" could perhaps be chest pains, and signal the "beginning of the end." I'm not sorry I called the paramedics that time, or the time after. What I see in retrospect is that my fears, fed by the ageism of the medical establishment, were in large part due to my ageist expectations that my body was supposed to give out.

That incident provided me with some first-hand education about the rampant ageism of the medical establishment. I was referred from one doctor to another, experiencing a range of attitudes from the paternalistic "what do you expect at your age" to the downright incompetent in which, despite all medical information that *less* rather than *more* medication is indicated with age, I was, without diagnosis, prescribed heart medication to take for the rest of my life "just in case." Only after I became very much sicker (from the side effects of the medication) and after many expensive intrusive tests was it determined that nothing much was wrong with me that could not be controlled simply by proper diet and exercise. Of course a part of me felt foolish. But the havoc created by this series of events impressed upon me as probably nothing else would have how crucially my own welfare depends upon my confronting and challenging ageism, the ageism of the medical establishment as well as my own internalization of it. I was forced as well to learn in a new way how I must indeed listen to and attend to my body.

Medical research shows that there is no reason that most of us cannot remain in relatively good health until all but the very last stages of life, particularly if we take proper care of our bodies. With age our bodies do demand more time and attention, and for the most part we learn to live with that greater demand. Like any other stage of life, there is a downside to old age, and I believe this is it. For all of us, young and old, our worst fear is what will happen to us in the event of chronic or severe illness in a society without adequate universal health care coverage, with a medical establishment that is racist, ageist, and sexist to the core, and with disability a social stigma. We are all haunted by the specter of being warehoused into nursing homes should we become disabled through accident or illness and unable to care for ourselves. We are taught to hate and fear disability and the disabled, and our society has tried to isolate and segregate the disabled, both young and old.

In addition, given that old age in white western European culture is thought of as a disease rather than a stage of life, it is not surprising to find that problems of living arising from greater fragility are reduced to medical problems requiring medical solutions. The medicalization of old age means that government funding gets funnelled through the medical establishment into nursing homes, vastly more expensive for the consumer and vastly more profitable for the provider than home health care.

The whole issue of possible disability raises another new area for reevaluating long held beliefs and attitudes. I have worked hard to become self-reliant and independent, and my ability to be "my own" person and do it "on my own" has been a source of pride for me. Lesbians, who do not look to men to be taken care of, place a high premium on that quality and have much difficulty in asking for help. Now, as an old woman, I am forced to reexamine the value I have placed upon personal independence at the expense of interdependence.There is much stretching to do in knowing that I am not diminished by asking for help. Should I become chronically disabled, I know I will face more critically the ongoing struggle to maintain an intact sense of myself while relying more upon others.

One thing is certain, our society makes interdependence difficult, for we live in a society segregated by race, ethnicity and age. Before I became conscious of my own ageism, I assiduously avoided anything that had to do with "old," including activities at our local Senior Center. As I began to acknowledge and accept my aging, I also began eagerly to seek out the companionship of old women, in my local neighborhood and in the lesbian community. It didn't take me long to know that the best of my learning and growth could take place here with these old women, as together we confronted the gripping issues of our lives.

Without any apparent loss of the energy and excitement of my youth, I once again became an activist, as one of the founders and organizers of the First West Coast Conference and Celebration of Old Lesbians (1987), as well as of the national Old Lesbians Organizing for Change (OLOC), which grew out of the Second West Coast Conference in San Francisco (1989). Lesbians, this time old lesbians, are once again in the forefront, on the cutting edge of the struggle for women's liberation.

We did an enormous amount of hard work to clarify our purpose and our goals as we hammered out a policy to confront the ageism within our lesbian community as well as the larger community. The uncompromising nature of our struggle was set from the start when we limited our group to old lesbians sixty and over, and when we insisted on calling ourselves OLD. The age limit exists so that old women have the opportunity to speak for ourselves, for, as an OLOC brochure (1992) says, "we are especially sensitive to those who see themselves as committed to the old, doing 'good' for the old, speaking for us. That is ageism!"

The insistence, for the first time, on 60 as an exclusive limit for belonging made 60 plus an important and empowering time in women's lives. I pointed out in my welcoming talk at the First West Coast Conference that important and painful as the problems of mid-life women may be, "to lump aging from 40 to 90+ is once again to trivialize the problems of old women–and once again to defer to younger women. We are expected to be available to nurture young and mid-life lesbians. Instead we boldly say 'No, this is our space.' We take this strong stand to affirm ourselves."

The "O" word is probably more dreaded than the "L" word. I have never yet attended a group, as either leader or participant in which the issue has not come up. Why use that word. I will never forget one group in which an old lesbian talked about how disgusting, revolting, and actually nauseating that word was. Yet we old lesbians again stood firm, accepting none of the euphemistic substitutes that came pouring in.

The OLOC brochure says that although "Old has become a term of insult and shame . . . we refuse the lie that it is shameful to be an old woman." We are neither "older" (than whom?), nor "elder," nor "senior." We name and proclaim ourselves as OLD for we no longer wish to collude in our own oppression by accommodating to language that implies in any way that old means inferior, ugly or awful. For to the degree that old women deny our own aging we cripple our ability to live. By naming ourselves old, we give up the attempt to pass. And as we break our silence, we empower ourselves and each other.

The excitement of this struggle is enormous. There were approximately 200 old lesbians attending each of the West Coast Conferences, and within a year when OLOC began to issue a Newsletter the mailing list grew to over 700 names. Now there are clusters of old lesbians meeting in at least 14 states, with plans for some of us to caravan around the country to meet and organize additional old lesbians. There is no question that old lesbians want to network with each other and share their experiences so that they can become a force in changing the ageism of our society.

Such an exciting endeavor! I often feel astonished at how rich in exploration and discovery my life is. This is not what I expected. This self of mine, that I always characterized at its best as a seeker after truth, is still in there doing her thing! And I am surprised, for I believed the same things we were all taught about what it means to be old.

I am learning better than ever before just how political the personal is. Never has my political life been so intertwined with my personal thrust toward clarity and resolution. I believe that our work has impact, that I have impact as we old lesbians continue to organize and make ourselves visible.

As part of our active engagement with life I and my partner are constantly building our friendship circle, a community of old and new friends and comrades, based first on our own special group of old lesbians but extending intergenerationally to many women. For our community of women strengthens and sustains us.

I have always wanted to live a mindful life, and I believe that my ongoing process of checking the dimensions of my own reality keep me mindful, alert and aware.

I am bemused when I think of my many fears about growing old. I was even afraid to retire and waited an extra year because I wasn't sure that I would have either enough to do or enough money to do it with. Although money is not abundant, I am fortunate that it is an occasional rather than a chronic worry. Since we hear only the down side of growing old, I was unprepared for my life as it is now. It is different from what I expected. Not until I stopped working could I even begin to imagine the exhilarating sense of freedom which unstructured open-ended time makes possible, a delicious experience I am having for the first time in my life.

How could I expect that my old age would be so full of life and love and excitement? All the ageist cliches depict old age as a static time, and the major gerontological theories reinforce those cliches, categorizing old age as a time of disengagement, when the biological clock winds down and the spirit and psyche withdraw. I do not dispute that such characterizations may be true for some. That is not the way, however, I am experiencing my life. I am not unaware that my body is moving closer to dying, and that at the time of my actual dying, if the process is natural and not precipitated by trauma, I may indeed have a different agenda.

For now, however, my life is very much in process, full of opening new doors while looking back at old and treasured experiences. My past gives my present a richness and a backdrop for the exploration which is happening in the present. Almost every value and belief I have held is up for reexamination and reevaluation.

In speaking of my old age, I once declared with some disappointment that I have not miraculously arrived at a state of grace or of wisdom, that I am still in process. This, then, is perhaps the greatest miracle of all. That so long as there is life, there is the possibility of growth and change. Old age provides no guarantees but death. However, it does provide us with a special gift, the final challenge and the final opportunity to grow up.

REFERENCES

Copper, B. (1988). *Over the hill, Reflections on ageism between women.* Freedom, CA: The Crossing Press.

Macdonald, B. & Rich, C. (1991). *Look me in the eye–old women aging and ageism.* San Francisco, CA: Spinsters Book Company.

OLOC Brochure (1992). OLOC, P.O. Box 980422, Houston, TX 77098.

Rich, C. (1988). Ageism and the politics of beauty. In Macdonald, B. & Rich, C. (1991) *Look me in the eye–old women aging and ageism* (pp.139-146), San Francisco, CA: Spinsters Book Company.

The Myth of the Golden Years: One Older Woman's Perspective

Marcelle R. Adolph

SUMMARY. Adjusting to old age requires more than coming to terms with eventual physical decline. It also demands accepting the permanent loss of loved ones. This autobiographical account describes both positive and negative experiences during the seventh decade of life. My coping skills have been enhanced by previous employment as a mental health professional. As an older woman, I have been forced to become my own social worker, acting on my own behalf with medical and other bureaucracies. And, as a retired social worker, I have the ability to evaluate the skills and limitations of those care providers who have been called upon to assist me in coping with the problems of old age.

According to the popular press, the Baby Boom Generation perceives age 40 as "over the hill." Inspection of contemporary greeting cards confirms this impression. Cards for 16 and 21 year olds suggest that these birthdays are cause for celebration; those for the middle-aged and elderly allude to failing memory, decreased sexual abilities, and diminished vigor and attractiveness, all in the guise of humor. Clearly, ours is a culture which considers getting older to be a cause for mourning.

Marcelle R. Adolph, MSW, is a retired psychiatric social worker who early in her career did group work with children and adolescents in settlement houses, youth centers, and a home for unwed mothers. Addressing the needs of adult psychiatric patients during the latter portion of her career, she was recognized as Employee of the Year by the major metropolitan medical center which employed her until retirement at age 70. Presently, Ms. Adolph serves on the Board of Directors of the Evanston-Skokie chapter of the National Council of Jewish Women and the Chicago Metropolitan Battered Women's Network.

Being told you look young is a compliment whereas wrinkles and sags are cause for depression. I can recall when one of my close associates in a women's organization told me that she could not believe that I was in my late 70s. After overcoming her shock, she told me that perhaps my curly hair made me look "younger than my years." I later learned from a mutual friend that this woman had coped with aging by having a face lift. A related experience took place at my orthopedic shoe store. While trying on oxfords, another older woman complained about the "ugliness" of comfortable shoes. She remarked: "My husband wouldn't let me in the house with these shoes; How could I wear these grandma shoes?" The poor woman had hobbled into the store with a cane, wearing silly little pumps. Her ankles, instep, and lower limbs were puffed up like balloons. She had been willing to cripple herself for the sake of appearing youthful.

Lest I give the impression that I am free of internalized ageism, I must admit that I continued to see myself as a middle aged woman (certainly not elderly) until I was in my 70s. Even now, I am reluctant to seek services or activities that are designated specifically for elderly persons.

When did I first come to terms with aging? When did I first realize my needs had changed? Age-related changes first became obvious when I retired from my career as a psychiatric social worker on my 70th birthday. Looking after myself and my husband became a full-time job; my life and self-image underwent enormous changes. What had once been identified as just normal aches and pains now was diagnosed as arthritis. Cataract surgery was necessary so that I could maintain my vision. I began to move more slowly; my sleeping patterns changed. The most enormous and traumatic change in my life was the onset of serious illness in my husband–a fast-moving, painful, and debilitating form of cancer which resulted in his recent death.

MOURNING AND THE AGING PROCESS

Prior to my husband's death and my 77th birthday, I had noticed that my arthritis had taken a turn for the worse. My internist prescribed a medication which combined a tranquilizer with a pain killer. The drug failed to relieve my symptoms. I then sought the assistance of a rheumatologist who diagnosed my condition as Polymyalgia Rheumatica. What a romantic-sounding name for a crippling disease! I could no longer climb stairs or turn in bed. My mobility was greatly impaired. Every part of my body ached; the pain was frightening. My late husband had to pull me out of bed and out of chairs. I was afraid I would end up either bedridden or in a wheel chair.

Shortly after a new medication enabled me to recover from a severe bout with my arthritic condition, my husband developed several medical symptoms. I was deeply concerned. He no longer seemed to have an appetite, coughing constantly and appearing to choke while eating. My husband was unable to swallow normally. His rapid onset of symptoms was swiftly followed by excessive weight loss. Always reluctant to seek medical assistance, I finally convinced my husband to be evaluated by a physician. He was hospitalized immediately, diagnosed with endema carcinoma (cancer of the esophagus). I asked my daughter to fly to Chicago to help us out. I was in shock, distressed about his rapidly deteriorating condition and worried about our future.

The medical team informed us that my husband had a very serious form of cancer and that death would be both imminent and excruciating without immediate treatment. Surgery was recommended but the prognosis was guarded. The typical patient with the kind of cancer my husband had lives only one or two years after removal of the esophagus.

According to the surgeon, my husband's operation was "a great success." He was told that he was fortunate to be able to return home in less than three weeks and was led to expect that he would be able to eat and swallow in a nearly normal fashion after a short period of time. I arranged for help from an agency that provides home care for chronically ill patients. Every day, a certified nursing aid came to our apartment to assist my husband and me. Care was expensive, and my daughter wondered out loud how long my husband and I could afford this service. The extended family was also anxious because before his illness, my husband had assumed many household duties that I was unable to do because of my arthritis. It became clear that I needed to employ a housekeeper regularly as well as maintaining the nursing aid service. All of this placed additional strain on my limited finances.

Within two weeks of his return from the hospital, my husband's distressing symptoms returned. He lost weight, no longer had an appetite, and began to choke and cough for hours at a time. He was unable to sleep sufficiently as a result of his deteriorating health. My nights were sleepless, too, as my husband needed constant care, and the nursing aid service was limited to the daytime hours.

The surgeon examined my husband once after his return from the hospital. He was diagnosed as having pneumonia but the medication he was prescribed only made him worse. Later, my husband visited his personal physician from our health maintenance organization (HMO). Although he was all skin and bones and could barely catch his breath, the internist declared enthusiastically: "Mr. Adolph, you look just wonderful!" I could hardly believe my ears. "My husband has pneumonia," I insisted. "Oh no," she replied following the most superficial chest exam, "He just has a touch of bronchitis."

I could hardly wait to get out of her office. Later, the internist called me at home to apologize. She had checked out my husband's condition with the surgeon and realized she had made a diagnostic error. I was enraged and wanted more than anything to tell this woman off. But, I bit my tongue, and politely thanked her for calling. This was one of many instances in which I experienced anger because the needs and insights of elderly persons seemed to be overlooked by those who controlled the health care system.

My husband's condition worsened. Instead of coughing up phlegm, he began to cough up vital fluids, bits and pieces of his own body. He suffered from terrible diarrhea and was humiliated by his inability to take care of himself. Finally, the Sunday before my husband's death, I called the emergency services of our HMO in desperation. I described my husband's continued deterioration. I finally reached his internist, doing my best to convince her of my husband's need to be hospitalized. In the background, my husband shouted, "I won't go to the hospital; don't make me go!" Instead of acknowledging that these were the words of a frantic man who never sought medical attention even when he needed it the most, the internist acted as if my requests for help lacked legitimacy. "There's your answer," she replied. "Clearly, your husband does not want to go to the hospital." It appeared that the economics of the HMO carried greater weight than did the medical and psychological needs of the elderly persons served by that organization. It simply wasn't cost-efficient to hospitalize my husband.

I could not accept the indifference of my husband's physician. I continued to argue with her, explaining that I could not manage him at home any longer. Finally, she agreed to allow a home care nurse to evaluate my husband's condition the next morning. The nurse arrived after another frantic night of caring for my desperately ill spouse. As I expected, the nurse knew she had to arrange for an ambulance immediately. After one quick look, my husband was on his way to the hospital. Never again to return home, he died four days later.

How can I describe the anguish and pain of seeing my life-long companion suffer and die so painfully? Had he lived a short time longer, we could have celebrated our 50th wedding anniversary and his 75th birthday. We held each other in his room; he comforted me while he lay there dying.

My husband's death came so quickly that our daughter was unable to fly back to Chicago in time to share her love and final farewell. At first, all I could do was talk to her on the phone. The hospital staff called me at 2 a.m. to tell me that my husband had died. They demanded that I come there immediately to help them with the necessary bureaucratic paperwork. Going there for the final time was terrifying. And everyone was so distant and professional, the setting so sterile and cold. I was asked to sign forms for death notices and other papers. No one was there to provide me with emotional support. But, at least I had a chance to see my beloved husband once more, to kiss him once more, to tell him how much I adored him, to say goodbye to someone I never imagined living without.

The next day I had to arrange for funeral services. To add to my pain and distress, my husband's sister announced that she would not join our immediate family in mourning. Extremely orthodox in her religious beliefs, she had decided that we (as Reform Jews) would not mourn my husband properly and therefore elected to "sit shivah" (or pray for him in the Jewish tradition) in her own home, with her own friends at her side and my immediate family left out of the picture entirely. I felt abandoned.

SUPPORT SYSTEM

During the funeral and afterwards, my daughter, brother, and his wife were very supportive. But, eventually they had to return to their homes in distant cities. I wasn't sure how I would handle my grief and new responsibilities without their assistance.

True, I still had a local support system. I received a great deal of continuing affection and assistance from close friends in Chicago, some of whom have been in my life for many decades. But, all their support didn't seem to be enough. I didn't think I could ever get over my grief. It didn't seem possible to go on without my husband.

I became extremely depressed, chronically anxious, almost in shock. I experienced an inner numbness, anger, loneliness. I didn't know how to fill my days at the same time that my life seemed overwhelmed with daily tasks. I was having difficulty coping. I was afraid of losing my sanity. I lost 25 pounds, was unable to sleep, frequently felt dizzy, and had a wobbly gait.

SPIRITUAL GUIDANCE

I was fortunate to have a compassionate and intellectually gifted rabbi speak at the services honoring my husband. My daughter convinced me to join his congregation to help me deal with my grief and loneliness. For the first time in my life, I attended religious services regularly. Judaism provided comfort as I began the mourning process, helping me renew commitment to life, assisting me in extracting a sense of meaning from the death of my beloved.

At first, the temple was the only place in which I could feel balanced and whole. I looked forward to shaking the Rabbi's hand at the end of each Friday service; his warmth, as he greeted each worshipper, was sustaining. After one particular service, I asked the Rabbi if he knew of a widow's support group. He was able to provide the name and telephone number of a social worker who anticipated beginning such a group.

I attended three sessions of the widow's group, but unfortunately, sciatica set in and I was unable to complete the six-week series, confined to my apartment by extreme pain. In hindsight, the missed sessions were not a complete loss. Group process had been disappointing. I was the most recent widow in a group which included women who had lost their partners one or more years ago. Initially, I had the fantasy that more experienced widows would show me how to regain good psychological adjustment. I was wrong. Apparently there is little truth to the cliche, "time heals all wounds." All around me were terribly unhappy women. Where were the role models I needed?

Religious services continued to challenge me psychologically and spiritually. I found myself becoming very depressed during one Friday night service. It had been a struggle to travel to and from the temple. It was cold and bleak; the rain had been pouring down in a deluge. After the Kaddish (the part of the service during which dead loved ones are recognized), I began to lose emotional control. It took all the strength I could muster to sit through the entire service. When the Rabbi asked how I was feeling at the end, I could barely speak. Tears rolled down my cheeks as I suppressed sobs. Rushing out of the Temple, I grabbed my very wet raincoat and hat. I simply could not control myself any longer. My stomach tied in knots, I screamed out my pain during the three block walk home. Crying profusely, I cursed my husband for leaving me to fend for myself in a lonely, cruel world.

I wanted to get through this pain on my own. So, when I got home, I elected not to call family, deciding instead to watch a frivolous movie on television about Knute Rockne, the famous football player and coach. Somehow, it was comforting to remember that Rockne had been a student at my high school. Oddly enough the film served a therapeutic end. I realized that I could nurture myself; I slept well that night for a change.

CRISIS

My life took a turn for the worse when an attack of sciatica incapacitated me just two months after my husband's death. On top of polymyalgia rheumatica (my form of arthritis), I now had additional pain. I could hardly move. Sobbing on the telephone, I cancelled a Thanksgiving trip to see my daughter a day before departure. Nothing could stop me from sinking into depression.

Thanks to two long-term women friends, I did not spend the holiday alone. But, after a delightful Thanksgiving dinner with their loving extended family, it was back to the reality of my aching body and empty apartment. Worse yet, I was too weak and disabled to be able to see my new therapist, a warm, skilled clinical psychologist employed part-time by my HMO. Home visits, even appointments longer than one half hour, were ruled out by budgetary restraints. Here as throughout the American health care system, economic priorities prevailed over the psychological needs and physical limitations of elderly patients like myself.

I was unable to walk to religious services, shop for myself, or attend organizational meetings. My telephone and the television became my sole source of social interaction. All the gains I had made in recent weeks seemed to erode before my eyes. Alone, I lost additional weight and slept poorly. I rarely ate a decent meal, becoming increasingly obsessed with my misfortunes. I found myself calling my daughter and brother more frequently, often several times a day and late at night. Although I sought their advice, their words failed to comfort me.

I was frightened, confused, and indecisive. I began to think about suicide. How could I go on without my husband? How could I manage with physical immobility and relentless pain? Didn't anyone care what happened to me?

Terrified, I called my daughter early one morning to tell her how upset I was. She recommended a brief stay in a psychiatric hospital to help me get out of my depression and begin to put my life back into perspective. I was very disappointed and let her know it. Initially, I had wanted her to fly back to Chicago immediately to be at my side. I knew she was very busy with her college teaching, but I couldn't help but feel abandoned. Didn't she know what an emergency this was for me?

In time, I came to terms with my depression. The belief that my daughter's personal presence would magically make my problems disappear was soon replaced with a more realistic one. I accepted my need for professional psychiatric help. This is no easy insight for a retired mental health professional!

I will never forget the Monday that I sought psychiatric in-patient status. The day proceeded like a black comedy. I was so helpless and distracted that my daughter had to repeatedly tell me exactly what to pack just in case I was admitted. My dear friend, another older woman, finally arrived to take me to the hospital. Because she had poor vision and could not drive on expressways, it seemed to take us forever to get to the emergency room. When I finally arrived, the nursing staff was unaware of my daughter's many long-distance telephone calls, informing them of my condition and anticipated arrival. Nobody seemed prepared to help me.

Staff at the very hospital I had served as a psychiatric social worker made it clear that since I was affiliated with a HMO, I would have to undergo several hurdles before I could be considered a potential psychiatric in-patient. First, I had to be relocated to another part of the hospital to be evaluated by a psychiatrist who was employed by my HMO. Before transport, they locked me in an isolation room without a chair to sit on. What a stressful place for an elderly woman who was crippled with arthritis and sciatica! As I was too shaky to walk to my interview, they had to escort me to my appointment with the psychiatrist by ambulance.

I began to cry profusely, complaining bitterly to the guard that I was being treated more like a prisoner than a patient. My bladder felt full. I asked to go to the washroom. But, the security guard insisted that I could not leave the room. I cried and moaned but to no avail. Finally, the guard looked at me anew and said, "I think I know you." Yes," I said, "I worked here for 19 years." When I explained I was a former employee, the guard relented and permitted me to go to the washroom.

Next, I learned I was completely on my own for the duration of this ordeal. The friend who had brought me to the hospital needed to return home. After a 15 minute wait, a psychiatrist called my name. Showing empathy for the stresses that I faced as a widow, he seemed to understand how difficult it was to live alone for the first time in my life, to be isolated from my closest relatives. He actively listened to my angry feelings.

Frequently, I was asked if I had a plan for ending my life. Although I was very emotional, I had to admit that my suicidal ideation was somewhat vague. "No, I didn't have a plan. No, I had never made an attempt on my life." Instead, I explained that "I just didn't seem to have a reason to go on living, that life without my husband was unbearable." I shared my death fantasy: somehow, painlessly, it would be possible to go to sleep and never wake up again. As depressed as I was, my capacity for rational thinking must have come through. "Mrs. Adolph," the psychiatrist explained, "You are not disturbed enough to be a psychiatric in-patient." Apparently, my HMO wouldn't pay for hospitalization unless I was stark-raving mad, dangerous to myself or others.

The psychiatrist suggested medication to alleviate my depressive reaction and suicidal thoughts. I was prescribed a low dose of Elavil. After our meeting, I felt much better. The emotional catharsis had a healing effect. I called my daughter to inform her that I had returned home, proud that I had managed a cab ride by myself despite the traumas of the day.

The night after my vain attempt to get hospitalized, I slept well. My conditioned worsened after I began taking Elavil, however. Soon, I found myself to be quite agitated; I could barely contain my rage. I pounded the bed and pillows with my fists. I was verbally abusive to my brother and daughter, calling them to inform them that they had completely failed me. The medication was making me crazy.

Somehow, I got the energy to complete needed errands, depositing and cashing checks and shopping for groceries. When I got home, I was still very agitated. I decided to wait it out. Again, silly television programs had a therapeutic effect. After two hours of viewing I was in control. I called my psychiatrist to inform him that I could not continue using the medication he prescribed. I was beginning to come out of the depression on my own; I preferred my own resourcefulness to the chemical complexities of medication.

SELF-HEALING

I don't want to give a falsely negative picture of what it means to grow old and especially to be widowed. The crisis of my depression was the precursor to a healing process. I have regained a sense of control and pride. I can see a purpose to living, loving, and relating as a newly single, older woman. Although my health problems and financial limitations cannot be ignored, they need not deny me access to independence or happiness.

I realize now that I was wrong to expect others to drop everything to look after me. I am at a point where I can accept help from friends and family while continuing to see myself as a resourceful person in my own right. How grateful I am for the love and assistance I get and receive from my warm support system. I think about one friend I have known for over 50 years in particular. When I was ill, this loving woman shopped for me, visited, and called regularly despite her own chronic health problems, restricted mobility, and economic limitations.

I am grateful, too, for everyone in my support system: the delivery man who brings me the groceries I can no longer carry home on my own, my landlords who look after every need of daily living and provide me with the continuing warmth of friendship, my many friends and loving relatives, and my vivacious cleaning lady who keeps my house tidy while rewarding me with ample hugs and kisses.

It is exciting; I am learning new things. For the first time in my life, I am in charge of finances. I am grateful to my daughter who helped me develop an efficient system for paying bills while arranging for a financial advisor to help me make prudent decisions regarding investments.

Various bureaucracies continue to present me with challenges. First, there has been the long process of negotiating with insurance companies and changing bank and credit accounts to my name. More frustrating is the continued deluge of bills and correspondence regarding my husband's medical treatment. Fortunately, my training as a social worker helps me deal with these hassles.

Writing this article has been therapeutic too, as have been continuing sessions with my clinical psychologist and psychiatrist. Although starting the paper felt like getting my teeth pulled without benefit of anesthesia, getting my experiences down on paper has facilitated insight and personal growth. I am glad that my daughter hounded me to write this; I am grateful to her for typing and editing my work.

Some of my memories are so painful and fresh. I have spent several sleepless nights as a result of writing–recalling the death of my beloved husband, my loneliness, and the pain of my illnesses. But, each day I mourn a little less and feel a little more alive. I realize now that loving and honoring my husband does not require me to give up the possibility of happiness. My background as a social worker helps me appreciate my struggles with aging, failing health, and loss. I am committed to the good fight of working through my grief while embracing life anew. Now, more than ever, I understand that activities, interests, and doing things on my own behalf are essential. I have rediscovered the pleasure of my own company and that being alone doesn't mean I have to be lonely.

Body Image Issues of Older Women

Joan C. Chrisler
Laurie Ghiz

SUMMARY. Psychological researchers have all but ignored body image issues of mid-life and older women, and medical researchers have limited their concern to the impact of surgery or chronic disease on body image. The purpose of this article is to point out that body image concerns are not restricted to eating disordered clients and can occur in women of any age. The impact of various aspects of aging on body image is described, and implications for the practice of feminist therapy are discussed.

Body image can be defined as "an individual's appraisal of and feelings about the body and its function" (Cornwell & Schmitt, 1990); it is the "internal, subjective representation of physical appearance and bodily experience" (Pruzinsky & Cash, 1990). Body image is an important part of our self-concept and, as such, provides a basis for our identity. It acts as a standard that influences not only the way we think of ourselves, but also our ability to perform various activities and the goals we set for the future (O'Brien, 1980). Although body image does not alter from day to day, it should not be considered "fixed or static" (Pruzinsky & Cash, 1990). It develops throughout life as a result of sensory and behavioral experience, physical appearance, somatic changes, societal norms, and the reactions of other people (O'Brien, 1980).

In recent years body image has become a hot topic in both the

---

Joan C. Chrisler, PhD, is Assistant Professor of Psychology at Connecticut College. She specializes in women's health and has written primarily about the menstrual cycle and weight-related issues. Laurie Ghiz, MA, is a recent graduate of Connecticut College. She is a reproductive health counselor and has conducted research on body image and compulsive eating.

67

psychological and popular literatures. Self-help books (e.g., Freedman, 1989; Hutchinson, 1985) are available in every book store to
help women learn to like their bodies. A search of the *Psychological
Abstracts* since 1975 turned up hundreds of articles examining almost every conceivable facet of body image–from definition to
measurement to its relationship to other psychological phenomena.
Most of these articles discuss the body image issues of high school
and college women, perhaps because the largest percentage of articles focus on body image's relationship to eating disorders and
because body image is thought by researchers to be most salient to
young women.

It Psychological researchers have all but ignored body image issues
of mid-life and older women. The medical researchers who have
investigated the topic have been primarily concerned with the impact of surgery or chronic disease on body image. So many older
women suffer from chronic illnesses that this is certainly an important topic, yet it is only part of a larger problem. Because of society's creation of a beauty culture and insistence that women pursue
an illusive beauty ideal (see Freedman, 1986; Saltzberg & Chrisler,
in press; Wolf, 1991), and because of the tendency to see youth and
beauty as synonymous (Alderson, 1991) and to define "woman as
body" (Greenspan, 1983), one can expect to find many mid-life and
older women experiencing body image disturbance as they encounter the effects of aging.

It may be difficult to feel comfortable about aging in a culture
where older women are rarely seen, and those who are seen are
celebrated primarily for their "youthful" good looks. In our society
"old" connotes "incompetence, misery, lethargy, unattractiveness,
asexuality, and poor health" whereas "young" connotes "competence, happiness, vitality, attractiveness, sexuality, and good
health" (Gerike, 1990, p. 37). We're told that we're only as old as
we feel, and the media drive home the message that women should
grow old gracefully by hiding the signs of aging. Naomi Wolf
(1991) interviewed editors of women's magazines who admitted
that signs of age are routinely "airbrushed" from photographs
through computer imaging, so that 60 year old women are made to
look 45. *Lear's*, "the magazine for the woman who wasn't born
yesterday" rarely publishes photographs of gray-haired women

(Gerike, 1990), and a content analysis (Nett, 1991) of *Chatelaine*, a Canadian magazine aimed at mid-life women, found that mid-life women were absent from the covers and the fashion and beauty sections and underrepresented in the advertisements. Although a recent content analysis (Vernon, Williams, Phillips, & Wilson, 1991) of prime time television shows found that more older people are portrayed as "more active, pleasant, and more involved than in the past" (p. 66), they still make up only 3% of all TV characters, and older men are generally portrayed more positively than older women. Ann Gerike (1990) has pointed out that only two of the Golden Girls have gray hair–Sophia, who is supposed to be 20 years older than the others, and her daughter Dorothy, who is "tall, deep-voiced, and powerful–clearly not the essence of traditional femininity" (p. 41). Nor are news commentators free from the media's bias toward youth and beauty. Christine Craft was fired from her job as a local news anchor because she was too old and too ugly, and it is widely believed that Jane Pauley was removed from her position as co-anchor of the Today Show to make room for a younger woman.

PHYSICAL CHANGES AND AGING

Despite the media's attempt to hide it, aging does change women's physical appearance. For example, the body's basal metabolic rate slows down with age, and is accompanied by a decrease in lean body tissue and an increase in fat (Rodin, Silberstein, & Striegel-Moore, 1984). A study (Young, Blondin, Tensuan, & Fryer, 1963) of a large sample of mid-life and older women found an increase in body fat after age 40. The mean percentage of body fat in women in their 40s was 23%; it was 46% in women in their 50s, and 55% in women in their 60s. Women tend to gain weight at each of the major reproductive milestones: menarche, pregnancy, and menopause (Rodin, Silberstein, & Striegel-Moore, 1984). Furthermore, weight may become redistributed during menopause, resulting in larger breasts and waist and increased fat on the upper back (Voda, Christy, & Morgan, 1991). To put it simply, women should expect to change shape as they get older.

The very fact of menopause, which usually begins around age 50, requires an alteration in body image. Whether the cessation of menstrual cycles is greeted with sadness, indifference, or relief it changes the way we think about our bodies. In addition, the physical signs that typically accompany menopause can affect body image. Vasomotor instability (e.g., hot flashes, night sweats) may make a woman feel that her once reliable body is out of control.

Research on the psychology of appearance has found that qualities of the face are the most important determiners of attractiveness, and that injury or illness that results in scarring or mutilation of the face and neck is the most difficult for people to accept (Bernstein, 1990). The American beauty ideal demands a smooth, soft, and blemish-free face, but skin changes that occur with aging make this more and more difficult to achieve as the skin of the face and neck becomes drier and starts to flake, loosen, and crease. Wrinkles or warts may appear on the face and "age" spots on the hands. In addition the hair may become thinner and grayer. The extent of these facial changes varies among individuals due to both genetic and environmental effects, but may be severe enough in some elderly people for them to worry about children finding them "scary" (Bernstein, 1990). Although the body image literature suggests that gradual changes in the body are easier to adapt to than sudden changes (Pruzinsky & Cash, 1990), such adaptation may be easier said than done for those women who have been closest to the beauty ideal. One can easily see the appeal to those who can afford them of expensive creams and lotions, chemical peels, and face lifts. However, when these products work they produce body image changes as well (the sudden kind) that can leave women wondering, "Who am I really?"

Other changes that accompany aging may require the use of devices such as hearing aids, eyeglasses, pacemakers, canes, or walkers. These affect both appearance and body experience, as do surgical scars, limps or stiffness resulting from injury or arthritis, and imbalance or other side effects of medications (Hyman, 1987). Such changes underscore the hypocrisy of the adage "You're only as old as you feel." Eighty year olds can feel like 18 year olds while sitting on a bench, but come face to face with the reality of stiffness, weakness, and uncertainty of balance when they get up (Bernstein, 1990).

Changes in physical ability lead to restrictions in social and personal activities, which often result in lower self-esteem (Roberto & McGraw, 1991) as well as alterations in body image and self-concept. Osteoporosis is an example of a common disease of older women that has physical, psychological, and social consequences. The fear of falling or the worry that simply coughing or sneezing may cause a bone fracture often leads to psychological distress (Roberto, 1990). Osteoporosis may also cause severe pain, disability, and physical deformities (Roberto & McGraw, 1991). The pain usually leads to restrictions in recreational activities and can make normal tasks such as cooking or shopping almost unbearable (Roberto, 1990). Similar changes in self-esteem, self-concept, and body image have been found in women suffering from rheumatoid arthritis and systemic lupus erythematosus (Cornwell & Schmitt, 1990). Body image disturbance was more severe in the arthritis patients and more clearly related to the disease process, as the women reported that their major problems were due to mobility restriction. Body image disturbance in the lupus patients was more closely related to side effects of their medical regimen, and they reported that their major problems were fatigue and avoidance of the sun.

Other health problems common in older women that can alter body image and self-concept are stroke, heart disease, hypertension, auditory and visual impairment, diabetes, and cancer. Cancer surgery, radiation treatments, and chemotherapy often cause disfiguring changes that require psychological adjustment. Researchers have described body image issues in head and neck cancer (Bernstein, 1990), intestinal cancer (MacRitchie, 1980), breast cancer (e.g., Kriss & Kraemer, 1986), and uterine cancer (e.g., Schumacher, 1990). Sexuality is a key component of body image, and it is an important issue to address when working with mastectomy or hysterectomy patients. Psychological sequelae of mastectomy (Kriss & Kraemer, 1986) and psychological and physical sequelae of hysterectomy (Schumacher, 1990) can have profound negative effects on women's sexual experience and self-concept. Body image alterations due to aging may affect the sexuality of any older woman, and may be most likely to do so after the death of her partner (Malatesta, Chambless, Pollack, & Cantor, 1988; Porcino, 1985) when she realizes that the double standard of aging may make it difficult to attract another.

Women are acutely aware of the double standard of aging, and therapists should not think that lesbians are any less concerned about it than heterosexual women (Dworkin, 1989; Hyman, 1987). In a study of over 600 people ages 10-79 Pliner, Chaiken, and Flett (1990) found that at all ages women are more concerned than men about weight and physical appearance and have lower appearance self-esteem. Those women who had high femininity scores were the most concerned about their appearance and had the lowest self-esteem. A study (Shimonaka & Nakazato, 1986) of over 900 people in Japan ages 25-99 found a similar gender difference in concern about appearance in every age group. The women had the most positive body image in young adulthood and the least positive body image in mid-life. In her interviews with 32 women ages 28-63 Giesen (1989) learned that single women were more likely than married women to believe that they were becoming more attractive and sexually appealing with age. It is not surprising that women who place less importance on physical attractiveness, are more positive about their self-worth, and generally believe that they can control events in their lives have the most positive body image at mid-life (Rackley, Warren, & Bird, 1988).

IMPLICATIONS FOR THERAPY

Feminist therapists should be aware that body image disturbances are not limited to eating disordered clients and can occur in women at any age. It is important to remain alert to the possibility of body image concerns and to encourage clients to talk about them. Therapists (especially those at midlife) must examine their own attitudes toward aging, beauty, and weight in order to be most accepting of their clients (Dworkin, 1989).

Clients should be reminded that the feminist slogan "the personal is political" is particularly important to women's conflicting feelings about age-related changes in appearance. In a society that devalues older women and a culture that has largely ignored them, it may be difficult to adopt positive attitudes, particularly at mid-life. Therefore, women should be encouraged to celebrate aging, to consider their wrinkles and gray hair as outward signs of inner wisdom, and to view themselves as survivors of life's challenges. Older women might find participation in the Older Women's League (OWL), the Gray Panthers, and programs such as Elderhostel to be empowering, and they should be urged to consider becoming involved. Poetry by older women that celebrates aging is now more available (Searles, 1990), and therapists might want to share this with their clients. Women of all ages should continue to set personal, intellectual, and social goals, and support groups can include rituals to help women acknowledge and celebrate their goal attainment (Patterson & Lynch, 1988).

Dance therapy (Unger, 1985) and regular exercise programs (O'Brien & Vertinsky, 1990; Riddick & Freitag, 1984) have been found to improve the self-esteem and body image of older women. Therapists can also use any of the techniques that have been found helpful with younger women with body image disturbances, such as the use of journals (Hutchinson, 1982), visualization and guided imagery exercises (Freedman, 1989; Hutchinson, 1982, 1985), and cognitive-behavioral techniques such as disputing irrational self-statements, cognitive reframing, re-evaluating cultural assumptions, and increasing positive reinforcements (Dworkin & Kerr, 1987; Freedman, 1990).

It is necessary for feminists of all ages to work against ageist and sexist oppression. By our personal and political actions we can decrease the invisibility of older women and by changing our attitudes we can begin to appreciate their unique beauty. Let us take to heart the words of Sarah Lairo (cited in Searles, 1990, p. 159): "Old Woman, You give me the courage to live my life in freedom. Though the vision of You is sometimes frightening, the laughter in your eyes dares me to live boldly."

REFERENCES

Alderson, B. W. (1991, March). *An overview of emotional issues faced by women over 50.* Paper presented at the meeting of the Association for Women in Psychology, Hartford, CT.
Bernstein, N. R. (1990). Objective bodily damage: Disfigurement and dignity. In T. F. Cash, & T. Pruzinsky (Eds.), *Body images: Development, deviance, and change* (pp. 131-169). New York: Guilford Press.

Cornwell, C. J., & Schmitt, M. H. (1990). Perceived health status, self-esteem, and body image in women with rheumatoid arthritis or systemic lupus erythematosus. *Research in Nursing and Health, 13,* 99-107.

Dworkin, S. H. (1989). Not in man's image: Lesbians and the cultural oppression of body image. *Women & Therapy, 8(1/2),* 27-39.

Dworkin, S. H., & Kerr, B. A. (1987). Comparison of interventions for women experiencing body image problems. *Journal of Counseling Psychology, 34,* 136-140.

Freedman, R. (1986). *Beauty bound.* Lexington, MA: D. C. Heath.

Freedman, R. (1989). *Bodylove: Learning to like our looks and ourselves.* New York: Harper & Row.

Freedman, R. (1990). Cognitive-behavioral perspectives on body image change. In T. F. Cash, & T. Pruzinsky (Eds.), *Body images: Development, deviance, and change* (pp. 272-295). New York: Guilford Press.

Gerike, A. E. (1990). On gray hair and oppressed brains. *Journal of Women & Aging,* 1(1/2/3), 35-46.

Giesen, C. B. (1989). Aging and attractiveness: Marriage makes a difference. *International Journal of Aging and Human Development, 29,* 83-94.

Greenspan, M. (1983). *A new approach to women and therapy.* New York: McGraw Hill.

Hutchinson, M. G. (1982). Transforming body image: Your body–friend or foe? *Women & Therapy, 1(3),* 59-67.

Hutchinson, M. G. (1985). *Transforming body image: Learning to love the body you have.* Freedom, CA: Crossing Press.

Hyman, J. (1987). Who needs cosmetic surgery? Reassessing our looks and our lives. In Boston Women's Health Book Collective, *Our bodies, ourselves: Growing older* (pp. 37-45). New York: Simon & Schuster.

Kriss, R. T., & Kraemer, H. C. (1986). Efficacy of group therapy for problems with postmastectomy self-perception, body image, and sexuality. *Journal of Sex Research, 22,* 438-451.

MacRitchie, K. J. (1980). Prenatal nutrition outside the hospital: Psychosocial styles of adaptation. *Canadian Journal of Psychiatry, 25,* 308-313.

Malatesta, V. J., Chambless, D. L., Pollack, M., & Cantor, A. (1988). Widowhood, sexuality, and aging: A life span analysis. *Journal of Sex & Marital Therapy, 14,* 49-62.

Nett, E. M. (1991). Is there life after fifty? Images of middle age for women in Chatelaine magazine, 1984. *Journal of Women & Aging, 3*(1), 93-115.

O'Brien, J. (1980, April 24). Mirror, mirror: Why me? *Nursing Mirror, 150,* 36-37.

O'Brien, S. J., & Vertinsky, P. A. (1990). Elderly women, exercise, and healthy aging. *Journal of Women & Aging, 2*(3), 41-65.

Patterson, M. M., & Lynch, A. Q. (1988). Menopause: Salient issues for counselors. *Journal of Counseling and Development, 67,* 185-188.

Pliner, P., Chaiken, S., & Flett, G. L. (1990). Gender differences in concern with body weight and physical appearance over the life span. *Personality and Social Psychology Bulletin, 16,* 263-273.

Porcino, J. (1985). Psychological aspects of aging in women. *Women & Health, 10*(2/3), 115-122.

Pruzinsky, T., & Cash, T. F. (1990). Integrative themes in body image development, deviance, and change. In T. F. Cash, & T. Pruzinsky (Eds.), *Body images: Development, deviance, and change* (pp. 337-349). New York: Guilford Press.

Rackley, J. V., Warren, S. A., & Bird, G. W. (1988). Determinants of body image in women at midlife. *Psychological Reports, 62,* 9-10.

Riddick, C. C., & Freitag, R. S. (1984). The impact of an aerobic fitness program on the body image of older women. *Activities, Adaptation, and Aging, 6*(l), 59-70.

Roberto, K. A. (1990). Adjusting to chronic disease: The osteoporotic woman. *Journal of Women & Aging, 2*(l), 33-47.

Roberto, K. A., & McGraw, S. (1991). Self-perceptions of older women with osteoporosis. *Journal of Women & Aging, 3*(l), 59-70.

Rodin, J., Silberstein, L., & Striegel-Moore, R. (1984). Women and weight: A normative discontent. In *Nebraska Symposium on Motivation 1984* (pp. 267-304). Lincoln, NE: University of Nebraska Press.

Saltzberg, E. A., & Chrisler, J. C. (in press). Beauty is the beast: Psychological effects of the pursuit of the perfect female body. In J. Freeman (Ed.), *Women: A feminist perspective* (5th ed.). Mountain View, CA: Mayfield.

Schumacher, D. (1990). Hidden death: The sexual effects of hysterectomy. *Journal of Women & Aging, 2*(2), 49-66.

Searles, J. C. (1990). Inventing freedom: The positive poetic "mutterings" of older women. *Journal of Women & Aging, 1*(4) 153-160.

Shimonaka, Y., & Nakazato, K. (1986). The development of personality characteristics of Japanese adults. *Journal of Genetic Psychology, 147,* 37-46.

Unger, A. K. (1985). Movement therapy for the geriatric population. *Clinical Gerontologist, 3*(3), 46-47.

Vernon, J. A., Williams, J. A. Jr., Phillips, T., & Wilson, J. (1991). Media stereotyping: A comparison of the way elderly women and men are portrayed on prime-time television. *Journal of Women & Aging, 2*(4), 55-68.

Voda, A. M., Christy, N. S., & Morgan, J. M. (1991). Body composition changes in menopausal women. *Women & Therapy, 11*(2), 71-96.

Wolf, N. (1991). *The beauty myth: How images of beauty are used against women.* New York: William Morrow.

Young, C. M., Blondin, J., Tensuan, R., & Fryer, J. H. (1963). Body composition studies of older women, thirty-seventy years of age. *Annals of the New York Academy of Sciences, 110,* 589-607.

Where Are the Archetypes?
Searching for Symbols
of Women's Midlife Passage

Valerie H. Mantecon

SUMMARY. What does it mean to women's souls to grow older in a society that values masculinity and youth? When a culture's language has no word to connote "wise elder woman," what happens to the women who carry the "Grandmother" consciousness for the collective?

This article examines our culture's male bias and androcentric attitudes surrounding women's experiences of aging, particularly the stereotypes and myths about menopause. From a perspective of archetypal psychology, a feminist re-vision of mythological portrayals of older women is offered, focusing on five specific figures symbolizing the ancient "Grandmother" archetype of the Crone. In addition, two important conceptual constructs, created by women writing on archetypal theory, are presented as female-defined models and perspectives of empowerment for women who are journeying through the soul-passage of menopause, entering the powerful "liminal" space of mature femininity, of becoming true elders.

I sit in the steaming blackness of the Sweat Lodge, feeling the damp and heavy presence of 14 other women. We have just finished a Native American Sacred Pipe Ceremony, and are calling on the Grandmother Spirits to be with us. I am feeling faint, not sure I can withstand the waves of heat assaulting me. We are sharing our pain

Valerie H. Mantecon is a marriage and family therapist in private practice in Orange County, California, with a Master's degree in Counseling Psychology. She is currently pursuing a PhD in Clinical Psychology, with an emphasis on depth and archetypal psychology. The focus of her writing and research in her doctoral program is on issues of concern to women.

of lives lived as women, offering our anguished voices to the darkness. The Grandmothers are being evoked as images of strength and comfort. I feel cooled by their presence, and endure.

Later that evening, our guide asked that the woman in our group who embodied the Grandmother energy and consciousness for us all enact the sacred ritual of burying the ashes from the pipes. The honor belonged to the oldest among us, a 54 year old woman of color who seemed surprised to be chosen through no other merit than having spent the most years on the planet. But she completed the ritual with great dignity and grace.

I, too, was both surprised and deeply moved that night by the honoring of the Grandmothers and the elder woman who held their essence. In the North American, middle-class, mostly white environment in which I live and was raised, I have very rarely experienced older women being treated with such unquestioned and straightforward respect. And as a 51 year-old woman who is just beginning menopause myself, the meaning of this experiencing of powerful feminine ritual within a culture not my own has stayed with me, raising some profound feelings and questions.

What does it mean to women's souls to grow older in a culture which values masculinity and youth? Why is there no word in our language to connote "wise elder woman?" What happens to the women who carry the "Grandmother" consciousness for the collective? Where are the archetypes and models of empowerment and respect for older women? These are questions this article will explore, looking mostly to the works of women to re-claim the power of naming our own experiences, and to re-vision archetypal psychology's theory of feminine psychology as it relates to women transitioning into the second half of life.

Gender stereotypes can be particularly crippling for women aging in a cultural environment that does not value us. One of the cruelest of these stereotypes is the "menopausal woman." She who is undergoing a profound life change and transition with the ending of her blood cycles and fertility. She who is stereotypically perceived in Western society as diseased and in need of medication (hormones and tranquilizers), emotionally unstable, and having lost primary usefulness in life. These are cultural myths far removed from the realities of women's lives and experience. These are, in fact, lies!

For many women the word "menopause" has become frightening because we have been taught frightening attitudes about it with an accompanying frightening vocabulary. Rosetta Reitz (1977) believes this has occurred because menopause has traditionally been defined by men (medical and psychological professionals) looking at the experiences of older women as not valid in themselves, but only within the context of women's relationships to men. This patriarchal perspective defines menopause as "abnormal," as a disease. In contrast, Doress and Seigal (1987) state that menopause is a healthy and natural event in women's lives, but that there exists in Western culture the "medical myth that menopausal women suffer a crisis or 'deficiency disease' for which treatment is needed" (p. 116). "It makes me sad," writes Christine Downing (1987), "to know that if someone speaks of the myths . . . of menopause, they mean the un-truths, the fallacies, the misogynist distortions" (p. 13). She believes that our culture's view of menopause as "symptoms in need of medical treatment is yet another domain in which the meaning of female experience has been defined by males" (p. 15).

This misogynist bias is also inherent in psychological theories taught by the academic structures that train mental health professionals, offering a limited and male-defined view of the psychology of women. In the field of depth psychology, in particular C.G. Jung's theory of archetypal experience and middle age, where does women's mid-life transition of menopause fit? Where are the "Grandmother" archetypes? How are they perceived and how might they be re-visioned and re-defined, named by women's definitions based on women's experiences?

In the second half of life, according to Jung (1961), individuals are able to further develop and individuate the "Self" concept, which he described as the "imago dei," the maturational result of the "hero's" journey. He divided the life cycle into four periods: Childhood; Youth (puberty to age 35); Mid-Life; Old Age. Christine Downing (1987), quoting Jung on the intrinsic meaning of the second half of life, writes: "The afternoon of human life must also have a significance of its own and cannot be merely a pitiful appendage to life's morning" (p. 9). Jung attempted, in the words of Samuels (1985), to "see the whole man" (p. 171).

But what of the whole women? According to Downing (1987), "Jung . . . had no particular interest in the specific ways in which women may experience the mid-life passage" (p. 9). Although in theory Jung valued the feminine, it was presupposed as being identical or symmetrical to the masculine. And as is apparent in the above description of the "Self," the images given speak specifically to male psyches and male experience. Yet, according to Polly Young-Eisendrath (1990), "great trouble and sadness can arise (for women) in importing male meanings and imaginings . . . into the central holding place of female psychology" (p. 165). This is, unfortunately, a phenomenon that occurs too frequently in psychological theory and practice.

Jung (1969) believed that archetypes and archetypal ideas are those images and associations that originate in the unconscious part of the inherited structure of the psyche, and that they have always existed as a link to humankind's spiritual past. But, as Annis Pratt (1985) has suggested, Jung interpreted those archetypes that he labeled "feminine" through an androcentric lens, according to male patterns and projections "which has eclipsed women's experiences altogether." She offers a further critique of Jungian thought, stating that within this theory "men have been associated with mind and women with nature (and) there has been a tendency to see women as extensions or even creations of male imagination" (p. 98). She sees a serious problem with this because "if women are taken as attributes of the male psyche or (as) representations of nature, the body and the chthonic are understood only as other in relation to male questers, (and) women cannot be (seen) as questers in their own right" (p. 98). Menopause is definitely a biologically embodied phenomenon, and the elder woman as "quester" has been lost to the "male-as-hero" myth of patriarchal consciousness and its theories of psychological development.

Doress and Seigal (1987), in contrast to Jung's four stages of human life-span development, posit that dividing women's development into three stages is more in keeping with the reality of female experience. These are childhood, child-bearing years, and years past menopause (the "Third Age"). All are associated with the physical realities of women's blood cycles. All, within the context of depth psychology, archetypally correspond with the Triple Goddess worshipped by pre-patriarchal cultures as the creator and destroyer of all life–the ancient and venerable female divinity embodying the whole of female experience as Virgin, Mother, Crone. And, according to Jean Shinoda Bolen (1985), this goddess figure still exists, lingering as an archetype in the depths of the collective unconscious.

With the advent of patriarchy and its imposition of a masculinized world view, however, the ancient myths of the Triple Goddess were altered, splitting the wholeness of the feminine divinity and re-naming the parts. These usually male-defined derivatives of once complete femininity live on as symbolic fragments and figures in what we know as classical mythology. Yet myths, writes Bolen (1984) "evoke feelings . . . and touch on themes that are part of the human collective inheritance," and when a woman feels that there is a mythic dimension to what she is experiencing, that awareness can touch her soul in deep and creative ways.

However, in looking to the goddess figures in mythology as archetypes that can serve as menopausal guides for mature women engaged in this life transition, it is necessary to look beyond and beneath the images of patriarchal mythology. In re-visioning archetypal theory, Pratt (1985) believes that we "must transcend what men have projected from within their own psyches as ultimate feminine archetypes (and re-evaluate) beliefs and practices that characterize women as outsiders in culture" (p.130). Lauter and Rupprecht (1985) suggest that if archetypes are to be truly useful for women, we need to re-vision them in ways that are enabling for women, seeking conceptualizations that are true representations of reality as women experience it, rather than as categories to contain women according to culture-specific stereotypes. We must, as Pratt (1985) admonishes, "disentangle feminine archetypes from the warp of masculine culture" (p. 19).

The archetypal figure representing mid-life, or the "Third Age" for women, is the third aspect of the Triple Goddess–the Crone. Once known to mean "wise elder woman," this word and symbol of mature, knowing femininity has been profaned by "masculine warp," establishing the stereotype of "malevolent old womanhood" (Walker, 1985). It is interesting to remember, however, that ancient civilizations perceived life and growth as cyclic patterns encompassing aging and death as part of the natural cycles of life. This non-linear, holistic world view led to the honoring of elder women as "crones," women who held the "wise menstrual blood"–believed to be the source of their wisdom–in their bodies as they transitioned past child-bearing into years of value and service to their communities (Walker, 1985). Yet both Western culture and depth psychology have associated this goddess aspect with death, splitting it off and labeling it the "dark side of the feminine," holding it (and the grandmothers of the culture) in contempt and convoluted fear. In denying the ancient aged archetype of the Crone her full embodiment and symbolism, patriarchal cultures and their psychologies also deny and devalue the elder women who carry the "Grandmother" consciousness for the collective.

In a re-visioned awareness of ways in which the Crone manifests in myth, what might we learn about women as elders? What inner images and insights might we remember? I will view, through a feminine lens, five specific goddess figures from mythology, listening for the echos of the strength and essence of the Grandmother archetype of the Crone in her pre-patriarchal embodiment of powerful and wise femininity. These symbols, metaphors for women's multi-dimensional ways of being in the world, can be empowering models and guides for women who are moving toward and through menopause. I have chosen the following Crone archetypes, all misunderstood or de-valued by current male-centered interpretations of mythology, because they seem particularly symbolic and useful to women entering this powerful "liminal" landscape. Because of space limitations I have given brief overviews of these archetypal figures, but I invite readers to explore their rich stories and legacy in more depth.

Hecate: One of the oldest versions of female divinity, Hecate, whose name was formed from the Egyptian root "heq," meaning "intelligence," was perceived by the Greeks as "the Crone form of the Mother of the Gods" (Walker, 1985). She was envisioned as inhabiting the Underworld as "Queen of the Shades . . . the 'Divine Grandmother' . . . the source of 'hekau,' the 'words of power' that commanded and decided all things, including the forces of creation and destruction" (p. 50). The ancient people who originally worshipped her called her "most lovely one," calling on her power to protect women in childbirth (Walker, 1985). Hecate, in her Crone aspect, is "associated with thresholds and crossroads, with transitions and transformations" (Downing, 1987, p. 43). As archetype of elder woman, Hecate can be perceived as a powerful guide for women at mid-life who are crossing the threshold into the "Grandmother" transformation.

Kali: Still currently worshipped in India, this goddess figure has been grossly misunderstood by Westerners as the "Terrible Mother/ Destroyer." Jung (1969) himself spoke of the "dark world of Hecate and Kali, which is a horror to any intellectual man" (p. 100). This illustrates the bias and fear underlying the androcentric viewpoint and theory in which the Crone archetype has been mis-labeled and projected into the psychology of women. In Hindu belief, there is no splitting of the goddess, and Kali represents the multiplicity of feminine power, the "primal creative principle underlying the cosmos" (Mookerjee 1988, p. 11). In further describing this goddess energy, Mookerjee writes: "The challenge of the feminine force . . . has been ignored and distorted by an extreme phallic culture" (p. 8), yet "the bird of the spirit of humanity cannot fly with one wing" (p. 27). Kali's "warrior aspect," symbolizing her ability to protect and create change, has been interpreted by Westerners as "cruel and horrific," yet Kali is . . . the archetypal image of birth and death, giver (and) absorber of life" (Mookerjee, 1988, p. 62). Hindus believe we are presently living in the "Kali Age," the time of resurgence of the divine feminine spirit, a time when the essence of this goddess, embodied in mature women, has the potential to "restore to our natures that divine feminine spirituality we have lost" (Mookerjee, 1988, p. 9). And perhaps also to restore balance to the world collective that has too long been trying to "fly with one wing."

Persephone: This goddess figure was, like Kali, seen as a Death Goddess from the beginning. The Crone form of the Triple Goddess Demeter, she was, according to Barbara Walker (1983) "far older than the Eleusian myth of classical writings." Persephone, often confused with Kore, was "Queen of the Underworld long before there was a masculinized Pluto" (p. 786). Possibly her rape and abduction as Maiden in the classical myth of Demeter and Persephone was a metaphor for patriarchy's conquest of Goddess-worshipping cultures. Yet this goddess image remains a powerful symbol of feminine transformation. Naomi Ruth Lowinsky (1991) describes this Greek version of Persephone transforming into her power in maturity as the archetype of "Persephone Rising," which carries a powerful message to older women who have left their maidenhood in the underworld of memory and in the lives–both lived and yet to be–of their daughters and granddaughters. Older women can, as did Persephone, grow into our power.

Hestia: Worshipped by the Greeks as Goddess of Hearth and Home, this archetype of "wise woman" offers insight and inner-centeredness (Bolen, 1984). Christine Downing (1987) envisions her as representing an image of femininity that is particularly relevant to women moving into and through our menopausal years, holding a "feminine generativity that transcends biological mothering" (p. 147). "There is something middle aged about Hestia," Downing continues, ". . . so essentially beyond marriage and childbearing . . . embodying assimilation and integration" (p. 138). As keeper of the sacred spaces of human living, Hestia can function as a "Soul Guide," providing a soul experience "available in the midst of the everyday" (p. 147). She reminds us of that aspect of the feminine which is hidden and often self-demeaning, yet can offer a "subtly powerful critique of our tendency to define ourselves in ego terms, by reference to our outward accomplishments and visible successes" (p. 142). I am reminded of how, in my experience in the Women's Sweat, the woman receiving the honor of performing sacred ritual was chosen not for her accomplishments in the world, but for living the longest, with the most accumulative experience in service to "the everyday."

Sophia: As the early Gnostic-Christian "Spirit of Female Wisdom," this alchemical goddess was a classic epithet of the Crone, "the Lady of Wisdom . . . Great Mother Sophia" (Walker, 1985, p. 117). As co-creator with God, Sophia represented the feminine principle of generativity and wisdom, the "Soul of the World." She was the female creative agent that was "excluded from the canonical literature of the Judeo-Christian tradition" (Singer, 1990, p. 230). Merlin Stone (1990) has noted that "wisdom has for so long been claimed to be a masculine attribute (that it is) one of the most difficult traits for women to believe we own" (p. 214). Images of wise elder men are very familiar. We call them sages, gurus, "imagos dei." Images of elder women, and the words that once meant "wise old woman" in ancient times–hags, witches, crones–have been distorted and profaned in what Lowinsky (1991) describes as the "demonization of the feminine," and with it the elder women who embody these images. It is necessary for women to re-claim the knowledge of our history–that which we have forgotten we once knew–the belief in our enduring and consistent intelligence, symbolized in the archetype of Sophia–our wisdom.

Bolen (1984) suggests that these goddess images "have lived in the human imagination for over three thousand years . . . as patterns of what women are like" (p. 21). They are archetypes symbolizing the Crone aspect of mature femininity, which can serve women as a Grandmother Guide, teaching us who we are becoming. Mary Daly (1978) encourages women to re-claim this powerful archetype and become "Conscious Crones," discovering in ourselves "depths of courage, strength, and wisdom" (p. 36) that are the birthright of women as elders.

In further exploring constructs of mature femininity within archetypal psychology, I have found two concepts that are especially empowering when viewed as models for understanding and honoring women's processes of aging. These are Genia Haddon's concept of "Yang Femininity," and Naomi Ruth Lowinsky's concept of the "Motherline."

Yang Femininity: This is, simply, "womb power." Haddon (1990) comments that "in a culture where femininity is (rigidly) defined as yin, women are conditioned to neglect their yang energy" (p. 249). She views the womb as being more than just a passive, gestating receptacle, describing it as "the organ that pushes forth mightily in birthing" (p. 246). This is a powerful and innately natural source of women's active, assertive strength. Yang-Femininity has remained "un-named, repressed, banished, relegated to the shadow" (p. 247), yet the concept contains within it the inclusive quality of "both/and," instead of the linear "either/or," and illustrates "an egalitarian rather than hierarchical relationship . . . creating a consciousness at home in multiple contexts" (p. 256).

This is an extremely exciting and useful concept for women at menopause. This is also in contrast to prevailing theory (eg. Jung, 1961; Strahn, 1990) that at this time in a woman's life, her increasing potential for actively assertive energy becomes more "masculine," more "phallic." I believe this "phallic energy" viewpoint contributes to the rigid limitations of gender stereotypes of Jung's psychological theory–"logos" as masculine, "eros" as feminine. Yet at the time in a woman's life cycle when her womb no longer carries the possibility or responsibility of nurturing new life, Yang-Femininity provides a model for envisioning the holding within and re-directing the force of this primal female energy, using it to birth ourselves into the third cycle of our lives–into our future. Women with developed Yang-Femininity are able to push from within the contexts and realities of this cycle of our lives, "bringing forth newness by the fullness of time" (p. 253). In essence creating and birthing ourselves!

The Motherline: Naomi Ruth Lowinsky (1990) offers this concept of female experience of continuity, originating from listening to the stories of women in the middle of their lives, as a way for women to understand and value ourselves through understanding and valuing our female lineage. This is the experience of "oneness of body and psyche" that is a "central organizing principle in the psyche of women" (p. 134). Jung and Kerenyi (1963) have suggested that the mother-daughter bond transcends generations, and that each woman's essence extends backwards into her mother and forward into her daughter. Yet women's Motherlines have been profaned by generations of "patriarchal appropriation," which have "taken over the power of the Feminine and separated women from their embodied source of meaning" (Lowinsky, 1990, p. 93). Women have been "torn from (our) feminine selves by a patriarchal culture in which women lose (our) identities . . . our very names, and become the possessions of men" (p. 91). Lowinsky believes that "women . . . out of touch with their Motherlines are lost souls" (p. 91). Women at mid-life, whose mothers may be nearing the end of their days, and whose daughters are becoming grown women and mothers themselves, are caught up in the process of changing places in the generations, in the collectivity of femininity. The Motherline is an extremely powerful and important model for "matriarchal consciousness"–honoring the sacredness of women's blood connections–that is deeply symbolic for women who, at menopause, are in the process of this profound archetypal shift. Learning a feminine "naming" of this phenomenon can be tremendously empowering–a way for the soul to find its way home.

I believe that within the archetypes of the "Crones" of mythology, and the concepts of "Yang-Femininity" and the "Motherline," lies the transcendent function of the feminine, activated for women at mid-life. The importance of this soul passage is not recognized by the patriarchal culture in which we live, nor by most professionals trained in the institutions of this culture. We must therefore honor and name this experience ourselves!

Women at menopause are growing into "Grandmother" consciousness–a true opportunity to be wise elders, the "Crones" of our communities. We are the models for our younger sisters and our children, who will look to us to embody in our living the grace and power of feminine aging. But in order to successfully complete this transition within the current social context, we must first re-claim trust in ourselves and in the wisdom of our bodies and our life cycles. We must re-discover and re-define for ourselves strong feminine models–archetypes symbolizing mature femininity. These are our guides to understanding the truth and sacredness of our lived experience, seen from the perspective of our own middle years, integrating a long view backwards with our vision of the future. Women have been "sitting in the dark" too long. Yet, not unlike the women who sat with me in the warm and womb-like darkness of the Sweat Lodge, we have been gathering strength, enduring, grounding ourselves in the continuity of our feminine lives. It is time, at this life-passage, to birth ourselves out from the depths of the shadow, into the light. It is time to unfold the power of the long-missing, long-gestating "wing" of our feminine knowledge and heritage. Our children are watching. What visions might they see, through us? We are the windows to their future.

REFERENCES

Bolen, J.S. (1984). *Goddesses in every woman: A new psychology of women.* New York: Harper & Row.

Daly, M. (1978). *Gyn/Ecology.* Boston: Beacon Press.

Doress, D. & Siegal, P., in cooperation with the Boston Women's Health Book Collective (1987). *Ourselves growing older: Women aging with knowledge and power.* New York: Simon & Schuster.

Downing, C. (1987). *Journey through menopause*. New York: Crossroad Publishing Co.

Haddon, G. (1990). The personal and cultural emergence of yang femininity. In C. Zweig (ed.), *To be a woman*, (pp. 246-257). Los Angeles: Jeremy P. Tarcher, Inc.

Jung, C.G. (1961). *Memories, dreams and reflections*. New York: Vintage Books.

Jung, C.G. & Kerenyi, C. (1963). *Essays on a science of mythology*. Princeton: Princeton University Press.

Jung, C.G. (1969). *The archetypes and the collective unconscious*. Princeton: Princeton University Press.

Lauter, E., Rupprecht, C. (Eds.) (1985). *Feminist archetypal theory: Interdisciplinary re-visions of Jungian thought*. Knoxville: University of Tennessee Press.

Lowinsky, N. (1990). Mother of mothers: The power of the grandmother in the female psyche. In C. Zweig (Ed.), *To be a woman* (pp. 86-97). Los Angeles: Jeremy P. Tarcher, Inc.

Lowinsky. N. (1990). The motherline. *Psychological Perspectives, 23*, 132-150.

Lowinsky, N. (1991). Unpublished lecture. Pacifica Graduate Institute. Carpinteria, CA. Spring, 1991.

Mookerjee, A. (1988). *Kali: The feminine force*. New York: Destiny Books.

Pratt, A. (1985). Spinning among fields: Jung, Frye, Levi-Strauss and feminist archetypal theory. In E. Lauter & C. Rupprecht (Eds.), *Feminist archetypal theory* (pp. 93-136). Knoxville: University of Tennessee Press.

Reitz, R. (1977). *Menopause: A positive approach*. New York: Chilton Book Co.

Samuels, A. (1985). *Jung and the post-Jungians*. London & New York: Routledge & Kegan Paul.

Singer, J. (1990). Finding the lost feminine in the Judeo-Christian tradition. In C. Zweig (Ed.), *To be a woman* (pp. 222-233). Los Angeles: Jeremy P. Tarcher, Inc.

Stone, M. (1990). The gifts from reclaiming goddess history. In C. Zweig (Ed.), *To be a woman*, (pp. 204-216). Los Angeles, Jeremy P. Tarcher, Inc.

Strahn, E. (1990). Beyond blood: Women of that certain age. In C. Zweig (Ed.), *To be a woman*. (pp. 188-195). Los Angeles: Jeremy P. Tarcher, Inc.

Walker, B. (1983). *The woman's encyclopedia of myths and secrets*. San Francisco: Harper & Row.

Walker, B. (1985). *The crone: Woman of age, wisdom, and power*. San Francisco: Harper & Row.

Young-Eisendrath, P. (1990). Rethinking feminism, the animus, and the feminine. In C. Zweig (Ed.), *To be a woman*, (pp. 159-168). Los Angeles: Jeremy P. Tarcher, Inc.

From Edith Bunker to the 6:00 News: How and What Midlife Women Learn About Menopause

Phyllis Kernoff Mansfield
Ann M. Voda

SUMMARY. The purpose of this research was to study how contemporary, healthy midlife women perceive menopause and what their sources of information on menopause are. A nonclinical convenience sample of 505 middle-class women aged 35-55 (mean age = 46.6) from across the U. S. responded to the Midlife Women's Health Survey. Overall, the findings convey a somewhat disturbing picture of menopause. Notable was the absence of any sense of achievement or elevated status associated with becoming menopausal; a disease focus was common as well. These findings are discussed in terms of strategies to help women's adjustment to this life stage.

INTRODUCTION

Palovitch (1991) has shown that midlife women's responses to menopause are related to the meaning it has for them. In turn, the meaning of menopause for any woman depends in large part on the information available to her. As such, we might expect that contrasting portrayals of menopause as a deficiency disease or as a

Phyllis Kernoff Mansfield, PhD, is Associate Professor of Health Education and Women's Studies at Pennsylvania State University. Her work focuses on midlife women's health issues. Ann Voda, RN, PhD, is Professor of Nursing at the University of Utah. She is Director of the Tremin Trust Longitudinal Research Program on Women's Health. The authors are collaborating on a longitudinal study of midlife women's experiences during the menopausal transition.

normal life event would likely give rise to very different expectations and reactions to menopause among midlife women. The purpose of this research was (1) to study how a large sample of healthy midlife women perceive menopause, i.e., what meaning it has for them, and (2) to determine what sources of information they use in formulating their beliefs about menopause.

METHOD

Between March and May 1990, a 12-page Midlife Women's Health Survey was mailed to a convenience sample of 852 women between the ages 35-55. Surveys were returned by 505 women, for a return rate of 60.5%.

Measures

The Midlife Women's Health Survey solicited information from respondents about their reproductive and menstrual history; their health; perimenopausal changes; perceptions of their menopause; and their sources of information about menopause.

Menopausal stage (pre-, peri-, or post-) was determined subjectively. Participants who stated they were menstruating in a regular pattern were considered premenopausal, those who had reported changes in menstrual interval, duration, or amount of flow comprised a perimenopausal group, and those women who had stopped menstruating for 12 months were considered postmenopausal.

Of particular interest to the present study was a series of open-ended questions designed to obtain information from respondents about current attitudes and feelings about menopause, specifically, "Which changes are/were you most looking forward to at menopause?" and "Which changes worry/worried you most?" and why. Three questions asked about the formal and informal sources of their menopause information: "Where do/did most of your ideas about menopause come from?" "Describe what you know about your own mother's menopause experience," and "Describe the very last conversation you had with someone about menopause."

RESULTS

As Table 1 shows, the sample was decidedly white, middle class, highly educated, married or living with a partner, and employed outside the home in mostly professional work. Nearly three-fourths of all respondents (N=368) fell into the 45-49 age group, with a mean age of 46.6.

Table 2 shows that the vast majority of women categorized themselves as perimenopausal. Changes associated with the menopause were widespread among respondents. Menstrual cycle and other physical changes were most prominent (80.5% and 66.5%, respectively). Other changes, such as sexual response, PMS and emotional changes, were also commonly reported.

Changes Respondents "Look Forward To" at Menopause

As Table 3 shows, 75% of the respondents were looking forward to one change: the CESSATION OF THEIR MENSTRUAL PE-RIODS. Comments such as these were common:

> I'm looking forward to not having a heavy period each month. I'm awakened often for one or two nights each month due to heavy bleeding/clot passing. I also tend to become anemic.

> Less hassle! No cramps. Seems like every time I want to go camping, take a trip, etc., it is my period. And at least one day I flow/clot so much it is a real pain.

> Not having to wear sanitary napkins–why? Because I don't like the odor,and I'm tired of all the years of soiled underwear when I 'missed.'

> No longer menstruating. Having to clean up the occasional 'spots' is a pain (e.g., at night when the bleeding slips past the pad in back).

The next most common response was looking forward to NOTH-ING. Characteristic comments included:

> None. I dislike feeling old. I never was uncomfortable with periods and took birth control precautions to prevent pregnancies. What's positive?

None. I like having the estrogen flow naturally throughout my body.

None. I kind of like having a period. Something reassuring about it.

The third most common response was anticipation of NO MORE PMS, by 12% of the respondents. All other types of responses occurred infrequently.

Chi-square tests were performed to determine whether the likelihood of responding in a particular way to this question was related to a respondent's age or menopausal stage. Although no stage effect was observed, respondents' age was inversely related to the likelihood of mentioning one type of response, LOOKING FORWARD TO BECOMING FREER/WISER; the under 45 group was significantly more likely than the 45 and over group to answer this way (Table 3).

Changes Respondents "Worry About Most"

As Table 4 shows, HEALTH PROBLEMS was the most common worry. Comments suggest that respondents were most concerned about osteoporosis, breast cancer, and symptoms that might require a hysterectomy.

INCREASED MOODINESS was the next most frequent worry for this group, and several women expressed their fear of becoming what one woman described as a "typical . . . bitchy menopause lady." Women seemed to fear the possible harmful effects on their family life:

Mood swings–because of the disruption it could bring to family life with two preteen girls; I'd rather they have the mood swings than me!

I remember how hard to live with my mother got. God forbid that my family should have to go through that. I'm afraid that they aren't going to be spared.

The third most common worry was about HOT FLASHES. In some cases, women not yet experiencing them seemed to fear them more than women who had:

Table 1

Demographics of the Sample (N=505)

	N	%
Race		
White	500	99.2
Marital Status		
Married/Partner	407	80.8
Divorced/Separated	50	9.9
Single	39	7.7
Widow	8	1.6
Education		
Some High School	1	.2
High School Grad	3	.6
Some College	27	5.4
College Grad	178	35.3
Post Grad	295	58.5
Family Income		
<$21,000	19	3.8
$21,000-30,000	29	5.9
$31,000-40,000	60	11.9
$41,000-50,000	66	13.1
>$50,000	315	62.4
Age (Mean = 46.6)		
35-39	32	6.4
40-44	57	11.4
45-49	351	73.5
50-54	45	8.8

Table 2

Menopausal Status of Respondents (N=505)

	N	%
Menopausal Status		
Premenopausal (menstruating in regular pattern)	87	17.3
Perimenopausal (menstrual changes noticed)	349	69.5
Naturally Postmenopausal (no menses for one year)	43	8.6
Hysterectomy	23	4.6
Taking Hormone "Replacement"	65	12.9
Experiencing Vaginal Dryness	117	23.2
Types of Changes Experienced in Last Year		
My Periods	349	80.5
My Body	290	66.5
My Sexual Response	211	48.6
PMS	209	48.2
My Emotional State	197	45.5
Hot Flashes	116	26.8

Table 3

Responses to "What Changes Are/Were You Most Looking Forward to at Menopause?"

	Overall	By Age		By Menopausal Status		
		<45	>45	Pre-	Peri-	Post-
No More Menstrual Periods (N=292)	74.9	73.1	75.3	76.1	75.5	64.0
Nothing (N=59)	12.9	15.3	12.3	11.2	11.6	20.0
No More PMS (N=55)	12.0	16.7	11.0	12.7	12.9	8.0
No More Birth Control (N=26)	5.7	1.3	6.6	4.2	6.8	8.0
No More Pregnancy Worries (N=25)	5.4	2.6	6.0	1.4	5.8	12.0
Becoming Freer, Wiser (N=16)	3.5	9.0	2.4**	1.4	3.7	8.0
End to Certain Health Problems (N=10) (e.g., Fibroids)	2.2	2.6	2.1	2.8	1.7	---

$**p \leq .01$

Table 4
Responses to "What Changes Worry/Worried You Most?"

	Overall	By Age		By Menopausal Status		
		<45	>45	Pre-	Peri-	Post-
Health Problems (N=94)	20.4	9.0	22.7**	13.8	22.1	19.2
Increased Moodiness (N=82)	17.8	23.1	16.7	27.7	17.5	7.7*
Hot Flashes (N=77)	16.0	23.1	15.4	18.5	13.9	34.6*
Nothing (N=67)	15.9	19.2	15.7	18.5	14.2	23.1
Loss of Attractiveness (N=53)	11.5	7.7	12.3	12.3	12.2	3.8
Weight Gain (N=53)	11.5	5.1	12.8*	9.2	12.2	7.7
Vaginal Dryness (N=45)	9.6	10.3	9.7	6.2	9.6	19.2
Getting Older (N=37)	9.4	7.7	10.7	10.8	9.2	7.7
Decreased Sex Drive (N=35)	7.6	7.7	7.6	10.8	7.6	3.8
Drop in Hormone Levels (N=26)	6.1	6.4	6.0	7.7	6.9	---
Hormone Replacement (N=23) Safety	5.0	6.4	4.7	3.1	6.9	---

*p≤.05

**p≤.01

I have heard horror stories.
I had been concerned about all the horrendous stories you hear of others' hot flashes, night sweats, etc. None of this really occurred . . . only a couple of 'flashes' that were more just long facial 'flushes' than anything else.

Worrying about NOTHING ranked fourth, while the fifth most common concern was over a LOSS OF ATTRACTIVENESS. Respondents were worried about various actual or anticipated physical changes:

Physical changes of the body. It's a negative image of a body 'drying up.'
Weight gain is a constant struggle. I walk 10-20 miles each week and watch my diet but it's a constant struggle."
Body changes. Loss of youthful appearance. Fifty is too young to be 'old.' I fear beginning to look like my mother with a very large stomach.
Wrinkling, pot-belly, old-looking skin.
Getting matronly looking, gaining weight and looking thick; losing sexual appeal.
I would not like to take on any masculine characteristics as a result of hormonal changes . . .

Certain changes were more worrisome to older than younger women, or to women at one menopausal stage than another. For instance, older women (45+) were significantly more concerned with HEALTH PROBLEMS and WEIGHT GAIN than were younger women, while premenopausal women were the most concerned with MOODINESS and postmenopausal women, with HOT FLASHES.
Since the attitudes and perceptions about menopause expressed by these respondents are to a large extent a product of the information available to them on this topic, we then requested respondents to let us know from where or whom they obtained information. Table 5 lists respondents' answers to the question, "Where do/did most of your ideas about menopause come from?" From FRIENDS was the most common reply (39.8%), followed by BOOKS (32.8%) and MAGAZINES (32.5%). MOTHER ranked fourth which was

Table 5

Sources of Information About Menopause

	N	%
Friends	201	39.8
Books	166	32.8
Magazines	164	32.5
Mother	141	27.9
Physician/Health Professional	82	16.2
Other Family Members	32	6.3

ahead of PHYSICIANS/OTHER HEALTH CARE PROVIDERS
and OTHER FAMILY MEMBERS.

Some women expressed satisfaction with the available material
on the topic of menopause, although many did not. Selected comments representing both viewpoints follow:

> Women's health books and vitamin therapy books . . . were
> useful to me.
> Our Pastor taught a seminar with handouts to men and
> women which covered all this and was wonderful preparation.
> I have taken out every book in our small town library about
> menopause. None really answered all my questions.
> A friend (who is a *nurse-practitioner* at a major NYC hospi-
> tal) asked *me* about info on menopause!

Many women identified television shows, even comedy shows,
as a major source of their menopause information:

> I . . . listen to professionals on TV shows such as talk shows,
> newscasts, health specialists.

> Lately I find myself seeking . . . a TV program which might give information.
> Edith Bunker's menopause episode of 'All in the Family.'

Comments made by the respondents clarified the low rankings of MOTHER and PHYSICIAN as resources. Several women stated that their mothers did not provide them with any information:

> My mother told me nothing about the menstrual cycle or menopause. It was hush-hush.
> Very little was said about it at the time and my mother is very reluctant to discuss health or emotional problems which is part of the reason I sought counseling myself.
> I can talk about my experience today but we never did about hers, years ago.

In fact, fully one quarter (26.5%) of the respondents stated that they knew *nothing* about their own mothers' menopause experience. One reason was the silence surrounding the topic, as seen above. However, another reason had to do with the unavailability of mothers, either because the respondent was absent during her mother's menopause experience, or the respondent's mother was no longer alive at the time of the respondent's menopause:

> Unfortunately none. I was away at college at that time. She never spoke about it. I never asked. She died three years ago, before it became a concern to me.

Comments about physicians are suggestive of reasons this resource may have ranked low on the list for these women:

> Certainly not from the medical profession. Two doctors told me when I asked about when to expect menopause, 'Ask your mother.' Thanks anyway.
> Health professionals treat women like cars on an assembly line.
> Most health professionals do not feel comfortable or are not knowledgeable about menopause.

The importance of friends to these respondents was demonstrated not only by their high ranking as a source of menopause information but also by the responses given to the question, "Describe the last conversation you had with someone about menopause." Respondents were far more likely to talk to FRIENDS (53.7%) than to anyone else; they also talked to FAMILY MEMBERS occasionally (22.1%), but to CO-WORKERS or PHYSICIANS less often. The general topic of MENOPAUSE was the most common subject of these conversations (cited by 34.8% of respondents), with hot flashes a close second (29.2%).

Although 84% of the respondents reported that it was "very easy" or "fairly easy" to talk about their midlife changes and menopause, the open-ended comments describing these conversations are more ambiguous, suggesting both ease and discomfort:

> We always joke that we can hardly wait.
> Jokes relating to wishing menopause was here. Sick of having the period.
> Laughing at the office about hot flashes.

DISCUSSION

Findings from this study provide insights into both the beliefs and attitudes of contemporary midlife women regarding menopause and the sources of these perceptions. From first-hand descriptions of what these women were "most looking forward to" and "most worried about," we were able to construct the following picture of middle-aged women's perceptions of the menopause experience.

First, five of the six perceived benefits of the menopause represent the termination of current, undesirable conditions. Only one benefit, expecting to feel freer and wiser, represents a real advantage in becoming postmenopausal and even that declined among the older women. We see that contemporary midlife women, even when highly educated, still are influenced by physicians' and the media's negative portrayals of older women (McKeever, 1991).

Many of the concerns expressed by these women, e.g., the fear of becoming a "typically . . . bitchy menopausal lady," reflect the sexist and ageist stereotypes of aging that have been featured in popular articles about menopause since the 1960s (Chrisler, Torrey, & Matthes, 1991) and that women themselves have incorporated into their thinking (see Barbara Macdonald, (1983), for a poignant description of the author's painful discovery that even her young feminist 'sisters' were ageist). As long as women are valued primarily for youthful attractiveness, they will fear natural, even health-promoting body changes, e.g., weight gain and/or a redistribution of body weight, as threats to their femininity and desirability (Voda, Christy & Morgan, 1991).

A disease perspective of menopause was evident among respondents, whose primary worry was developing certain diseases of older age, e.g., osteoporosis and cancer. Not surprisingly, more older than younger women expressed this concern. Berkun (1986) also found "physical deterioration" to be a major worry. Since menopause still is portrayed as a hormone deficiency disease by both the media and the medical profession (MacPherson, 1981, 1985; Voda & George, 1986), these women are simply reflecting what they have been taught. Martin (1988) explains that this disease metaphor has been perpetuated by medical language that depicts menopause as a process of physiological breakdown; thus, ovaries 'fail,' 'atrophy,' 'shrink,' and so on.

The most commonly cited benefit of menopause by far was an end to menstrual bleeding, underscoring its salience in women's lives, especially because of the very heavy periods experienced by many perimenopausal women (Voda and Mansfield, 1992). This finding has implications for women's compliance with hormone replacement regimens, since the recommended addition of progesterone to estrogen for protection against endometrial cancer induces a monthly period.

Perhaps the most distressing aspect of this study's findings relates to the serious shortage of accurate information about menopause and the determined yet unsuccessful attempts of midlife women to acquire such knowledge. Their reliance on such resources as TV news broadcasts and even comedy shows such as All In the Family for information about menopause highlights their neediness. Other studies (Berkun, 1986; Mansfield, Theisen, & Boyer, 1992; Masling, 1988) have found women facing similar obstacles.

Nearly half of the women in this study received most of their information about menopause from their friends. Although the researchers acknowledge the value of informal support networks in working through challenging life situations, and as a source of information, reliance on friendships in this instance may have been problematic, for two reasons. First, 'joking' appeared to be an underlying theme in the discussions with friends, suggesting embarrassment or discomfort with the topic that might actually have perpetuated negative stereotypes. On the other hand, joking might be a first step to breaking down the stigma surrounding this topic. Second, many of the discussions with friends were short on solid information. Cooksey, Imle and Smith (1991) stress the importance of having "comparators" (p. 89), individuals such as friends or a mother, who can help women make sense of their menopause experience. They, like the present authors, found mothers to be absent for such purposes.

CONCLUSIONS AND RECOMMENDATIONS

This study provides us with a somewhat disturbing picture of contemporary midlife women's perceptions of menopause. Notable was the absence of any sense of achievement, or gained status, associated with becoming menopausal. Since women's responses to menopause have been found to be based on the meaning it has for them (Palovitch, 1991), one can speculate that the negative concepts of menopause held by the women in the present study may in the long run adversely affect their adjustment to menopause. Thus, it is crucial that we create strong positive images of midlife women in the media to serve as role models and continue efforts to eradicate from our society those sexist and ageist attitudes that give rise to such stereotypes in the first place.

At the same time, women can be empowered through education and support. Dickson (1990) proposes that free, open discussions with women about their experiences at the time of menopause can lead to questioning the assumptions which science and medicine have used to define menopause as a disease. Such questioning will result in the emergence of a new, woman-centered knowledge. Theisen's (1992) participatory research study groups for perimenopausal women demonstrated that discussion groups do result in the emergence of both new knowledge and strategies for action.

A commitment to this three-pronged approach–destigmatizing the topic of menopause, insisting on the creation of positive imagery related to aging, and making available information and support concerning the normal events of the perimenopausal transition–is crucial to enhancing women's adjustment at this life stage.

REFERENCES

Berkun, C. (1986). In behalf of women over 40: Understanding the importance of the menopause. *Social Work, 378*-384.

Chrisler, J.C., Torrey, J.W., & Matthes, M.M. (1991). Brittle bones and sagging breasts, loss of femininity and loss of sanity: The media describe the menopause. In A.V. Voda and R. Conover (Eds.), *Proceedings of the 8th Conference, Society for Menstrual Cycle Research, June 1-3, 1989* (pp. 23-35). Society for Menstrual Cycle Research.

Cooksey, S.G., Imle, M.A., & Smith, C.L. (1991). An inductive study of the transition of menopause. In A.V. Voda and R. Conover (Eds.), *Proceedings of the 8th Conference, Society for Menstrual Cycle Research, June 1-3, 1989* (pp. 75-111). Society for Menstrual Cycle Research.

Dickson, G.L. (1990). A feminist poststructuralist analysis of the knowledge of menopause. *Advances in Nursing Science, 12*(3), 15-31.

Macdonald, B. (1983). *Look me in the eye.* San Francisco: Spinsters/Lute.

MacPherson, K. (1981). Menopause as disease: The social construction of a metaphor. *Advances in Nursing Science, 3,* 95-113.

MacPherson, K. (1985). Osteoporosis and menopause: A feminist analysis of the social construction of a syndrome. *Advances in Nursing Science, 7,* 11-22.

Mansfield, P.K., Theisen, S.C., & Boyer, B. (1992). Midlife women and menopause: A challenge for the mental health counselor. *Journal of Mental Health Counseling, 14,* 73-83.

Martin, E. (1988). Medical metaphors of women's bodies: Menstruation and menopause. *International Journal of Health Services, 18*(2), 237-254.

Masling, J. (1988). Menopause: A change for the better? *Nursing Times, 84*(39), 35-38.

McKeever, L. (1991). Informal models of women's perimenopausal experiences: Implications for health care. In A.V. Voda & R. Conover, (Eds.), *Proceedings of the 8th Conference, Society for Menstrual Cycle Research, June 1-3, 1989* (pp. 232-255). Society for Menstrual Cycle Research.

Palovitch, B.T. (1991, June). Going through menopause. *Presentation at the 9th Conference of the Society for Menstrual Cycle Research, Seattle, Washington, June 6-8.*

Theisen, S.C. (1992). *Quality of life enhancement for women approaching menopause using participatory research.* Unpublished doctoral dissertation, Penn State University.

Voda, A.M., Christy, N., & Morgan, J. (1991). Body composition changes in menopausal women. *Women and Therapy, 11,* 71-95.

Voda, A.M., & George, T. (1986). Menopause. In H.H. Werley, J.J. Fitzpatrick, & R.L. Taunton (Eds.), *Annual Review of Nursing Research* (pp. 55-75). New York: Springer.

Voda, A.M., & Mansfield, P.K. (1992). *Menstrual bleeding in perimenopausal women.* Unpublished paper.

Women at Midlife:
Current Theoretical Perspectives
and Research

Lucia Albino Gilbert

SUMMARY. This paper considers changes in theoretical perspectives with regard to studying women. Findings from research in three areas illustrate ways in which emerging perspectives reframed questions about midlife women and, as a result, are providing myth-defying knowledge about the life experiences of women in their 40's and 50's. These areas are: women's diversity, women's health, and women and work.

In our society, 40th and 50th birthdays generate special celebrations and good-natured sympathy. There is a shared folk wisdom about the stress associated with these passages and a unique poignancy about the irreversible realities of aging. For women reaching midlife in the 1990s, these bitter-sweet celebrations of midlife are likely to occur in a context that differs considerably from women who were members of earlier cohorts. Because individuals at midlife are more likely to look to context than to age as a way of

Lucia Albino Gilbert, PhD, is Professor of Educational Psychology at The University of Texas at Austin and teaches in the department's doctoral program in counseling psychology. She has written a number of books, chapters, and articles in the areas of gender and mental health, dual-career families, and women and work. She is associate editor of *Psychology of Women Quarterly* and serves on the editorial boards of *Journal of Family Issues* and *Contemporary Psychology.*

An earlier version of this paper was presented in the symposium, "Gender struggles in the middle years," Arthur Kovacs, Chair, APA, Boston, MA, August, 1990.

Correspondence should be addressed to Lucia Albino Gilbert, Department of Educational Psychology, The University of Texas, Austin, TX 78712.

locating themselves (Neugarten, 1968), concepts of gender, and how they are changing, take on particular importance for midlife women today. Women who turned 40 or 50 in 1990, were born in 1940 and 1950 and thus reached adulthood during the time of the feminist movements of the 1960s and 1980s. More career opportunities and increased choices for women, made possible by the feminist movement and by changing social and economic conditions, affected their lives, if not directly, then certainly indirectly. Many of these women entered the workforce, initially with the understanding that any occupational work was in addition to attending to the needs of their husband and children. As Bernard (1975) noted, in the 1960s "It was easier (for women) to be for equal pay than for equality vis-a-vis husbands." Times continued to change, however, and during the period from the 1960s to the 1980s, the women's movement broadened its focus to embrace equitable roles with men in the worlds of work *and* family.

It is within this larger social context that this paper considers changes in theoretical perspectives with regard to studying women and how these new perspectives reframe how we look at midlife women. Findings from research in three areas illustrate ways in which emerging perspectives reframed questions about midlife women and, as a result, are providing myth-defying knowledge about the life experiences of women in their forties and fifties. These areas are: women's diversity, women's health, and women and work.

CURRENT THEORETICAL PERSPECTIVES

For some time now advocates of women's interests within the mental health system have raised objections to sexism in theories about women and in their diagnosis and treatment (Marecek & Hare-Mustin, 1991). Not only were women's experiences not well represented in psychological theory and research, but also when they were studied, it was with the assumption that male behavior was normative and that women were deficient or lacking in some way. Out of these early critiques and studies came the development of an extensive body of literature on the psychology of women (Wallston, 1981), the emergence of feminist methodologies (Marecek, 1989), and, most recently, the study of the construct of gender (Gilbert, 1992; Hare-Mustin & Marecek, 1990).

Gender and Its Theoretical Importance

The use of the term gender by feminists acknowledges the broader meaning typically associated with one's biological sex. Gender refers not only to biological sex but also to the psychological, social, and cultural features and characteristics which have become strongly associated with the biological categories of female and male. For instance, biologically women and men may both become parents, but only women typically were expected to rear and nurture children–a view somewhat prevalent still today. Similarly, biologically both women and men are capable of taking on leadership positions, but only men typically were expected to prepare for and enter demanding professional careers–again a view, albeit changing, still somewhat prevalent today.

The initial conceptual shift from sex to gender represented a dramatic change in assumptions about the causes of human behavior and hence in approaches to how best study and understand human behavior (cf., Unger, 1990). Psychological studies on sex differences typically derived from an internally determined or individual difference perspective which assumed that the characteristics under study, say parenting or leadership abilities, reflected an individual's essential nature. But as Sherif (1982) and others noted, biological sex forms the basis of a social classification system– namely, gender. Viewed from this perspective, many of the traits and behaviors traditionally associated with biological sex become *constructed by the social reality* of individual women and men. Take the example of differences between women and men in assertiveness on the job or in intimate relations with other sex partners. From a gender perspective women are not less assertive than men by nature but learn to be less assertive in certain areas and kinds of relationships because of societal prescriptions and expectations about women's behavior and what makes women desirable and acceptable.

Current theorists also see the influence and meaning of gender as extending beyond individual women and men and their interpersonal ways of relating to social structures and principles of organizations (Hare-Mustin & Marecek, 1990). As Sherif (1982) explained, gender serves as a pervasive organizer in our culture. A case in point is the proportion of women and men in the various occupational areas. Although women today clearly have more choices and opportunities than in 1972, the occupational distribution of women within the labor force has changed only slightly over time. If one considers all working women, and their distribution among all occupations, clerical jobs account for a larger proportion of employed women now than in 1950. Whereas approximately one in four working women held a secretarial job in 1950, approximately one in three now holds such a position (Spain, 1988). Thus although increasing numbers of women are entering the labor force, women and men are still typically found in different occupations (Spain, 1988) and women continue to earn significantly less than men (United Nations, 1991). The median income of college-educated women is still about the same as that of high-school-educated men. The reasons for this continued occupational segregation have to do with factors such as the differential status associated with traditional male and female behaviors and roles, women's and men's differential access to power and control of resources, and personnel policies that assume a traditional male model of employment.

Another manifestation of the gendered basis to relationships and organizations is the now well documented "glass ceiling," a barrier so subtle that it is transparent yet so strong that is prevents women and minorities from moving beyond middle management (Morrison, White, Velsor, & the Center for Creative Leadership, 1987). Once women break this barrier, which some women do, apparently they encounter still another unexpected barrier (Morrison et al., 1987)–a wall of tradition and stereotype that separates women from the top executive level. The "glass wall" keeps women out of the inner sanctum of senior management and off the male turf. The organizational forces which create and maintain these kinds of invisible walls and ceilings involve gender–sex discrimination, perceptions of women's and men's abilities, and discomfort with women in leadership positions.

Not surprisingly, women and men often internalize the broader "gender" meanings associated with their sex and may act in accordance with these internalized gender beliefs and stereotypes, consciously or unconsciously, in situations in which gender is salient. For example, laboratory studies on leadership tasks showed that women acted less dominant then they were dispositionally in their interactions with men, but not in parallel interactions with women (Davis & Gilbert, 1989). Similarly, women who experience sexual harassment in work situations, often blame themselves for the unwanted attention, most likely because they have internalized views of men as entitled sexually and otherwise and of women as accommodating to men's needs (Gilbert & Scher, 1989; Westkott, 1986).

CURRENT RESEARCH ON WOMEN AT MIDLIFE

One of the purposes in evolving feminist approaches to research is to facilitate the understanding of women's and men's experiences within their societal context and to construct nonsexist theories of human development. Sexism and gender bias characterize psychological research and theory to the extent that unexamined assumptions about the sexes or untested distinctions based on gender enter into hypotheses, rationale, norms of adjustment, or coverage of the field (McHugh, Koeske, & Frieze, 1986). This section identifies three areas in which gender biases limited or misinformed research on midlife women and briefly describes how emerging theoretical perspectives are reframing the experiences of women at midlife and the issues they face.

Women's Diversity

As Heilbrun (1988) noted in her book, *Writing a woman's life,* for too long we assumed all women had the same end, that they were indeed all the same, and thus needed no place or voice in literature and history. Treating women the same also characterized research and theory on women. Traditionally, women were viewed not only as deficient in "desirable" characteristics but also uninteresting to study because their lives were so predictable. This was particularly true for women at midlife precisely because women's lives ended when they married and had children. The only event left for them, menopause, in essence made women even less desirable to men and society. (Women's experience of menopause is discussed in more detail in the next section of the paper.)

Today researchers are much more committed to understanding the diversity of women's lives. There is a clear recognition of the heterogeneity of women at midlife–not only across groups (culture, race, and cohort)–but also within groups (cf. Baruch & Brooks-Gunn, 1984; Fodor & Franks, 1990; Giele, 1982; Hunter & Sundel, 1989). Some women in their 40s and 50s are peaking in their careers, others have returned to school after rearing children, and others are struggling as single parents in a competitive workplace for which they may not be prepared educationally. Still others are having a first child or are caught in the "sandwich" of caring for children at home and aging parents. And still others are choosing other women as romantic and sexual partners.

Women's Health

The major threats to women's health are the persistence of myths and stereotypes about women, particularly those associated with the gender processes discussed earlier, and the resulting lack of knowledge about women's health as they age (Rodin & Ickovics, 1990). The homogeneity and invisibility that characterized earlier psychological theory and research on women also holds true for medical research. Foremost here is the overemphasis on, and distortion of, the experience of menopause.

Rather then marking the end of a women's life, we now know that menopause presents few problems for most women; the "hot flash" is the only universal symptom. After menopause, women typically feel positive about this bodily change and many consider it a "nonevent" with the exception of not having to worry about pregnancy. The medical profession, however, has viewed this natural event as a deficiency disease. The widespread use of estrogen-replacement therapy began in the 1960s when pharmaceutical companies aggressively promoted estrogen as a wonder drug that would keep women young forever–a promise and goal entirely consistent with societal views of what makes women desirable. Current research indicates that hormone therapy may be useful for some women–women who have had their ovaries removed, women who experience menopausal discomforts, and women who are at high risk of fractures, but it is not helpful to ALL women (National Women's Health Network, 1989).

Also notable is the underrepresentation of women in medical research, again a situation which entirely parallels psychological research until relatively recently. Studies on health problems, such as breast cancer, that affect mostly women in the forties and fifties have received significantly less attention from researchers and much less funding from NIMH than life threatening diseases for men. In fact, one of the first acts of the current, and first female, director of the National Institutes of Health was announcing a new $500 million program of research on women's health, which will focus on causes, preventions, and cures of the chief threats to older women–cancer, heart disease, and osteoporosis (Eckholm, 1991).

A final concern, which also parallels deficiencies in psychological research on women, is the use of male subjects as normative or representative of women and men. Biomedical research on diseases that affect both women and men have typically used only men as subjects but results are generalized to women and men. The basic research on antidepressants, for example, was performed on male rats to avoid the estrus cycles. The biggest consumers of antidepressants, however, are women. A similar situation now exists with heart disease. It is only recently that women have been added to large scale longitudinal studies.

Woman and Work

Overall paid work benefits women's lives as does multiple role involvement (Barnett et al., 1987; Gilbert, 1988). Today more women are in the paid work force than ever before and women now constitute nearly 39% of the professional labor force; the large majority of these women are married and most have children. Other important changes are occurring. Foremost among these are the greater psychological expectation that wives will work and the greater significance attributed to work and career as a source of primary identity for women (Barnett et al., 1987; Giele, 1982). The benefits for midlife women are readily identified. They include the opportunity to have developed professionally and to have established a sense of self separate from a man and children, economic independence, and perhaps greater intellectual companionship and contentment. Because many of these women have both their occupational work and family relationships, even if divorced, to use in defining their adult lives, the typical midlife transition from active childbearing to the proverbial empty nest is qualitatively different. Rossi (1980), for example, noted that, unlike what was true for women twenty years ago, cohorts of middle-aged women show no elevation of stress compared with men their age. She speculated that this difference is due to the predictability of women's continuing employment. Similarly, Baruch, Barnett, and Rivers (1983), concluded that women, especially those in middle adulthood, are feeling better off because they are able to develop the "doing" side of themselves and to enhance their sense of mastery and independence.

Moreover, family and work issues interact in a particular way at midlife (Gilbert & Davidson, 1989). Whatever the decision made with regard to children–to have them early, to have them late, to not have them at all–at midlife the consequences of the decision are often reviewed. For women at midlife with children reaching maturity, there is the prospect of what might have been achieved had it not been for the family demands. For those who delayed childbearing, there is the challenge of dealing with adolescents or even toddlers while still struggling to preserve the career ground that has been gained. For those who decided not to have a child, midlife represents a finalizing of the decision.

CONCLUDING REMARKS

In summary, social change and changes in theoretical perspectives about women's characteristics and development are crucial to considerations of midlife women–the influence of economic conditions, of ideology about women's and men's roles, of the normative timing of such events as age of marriage and childbearing all influence women's choices and experiences. Women's lives can only be understood when studied within these complex social realities; and it is here that the conceptual shift from sex to gender, described earlier, has made a significant difference in reframing research questions about women at midlife.

Social changes appear to have had both positive and negative consequences for women at midlife (Baruch & Brooks-Gunn, 1984). On the negative side, for example, the sex differential in life expectancy is a biosocial phenomenon that greatly restricts the availability of partners of heterosexual women. On the positive side, the postponement of marriage and childbearing is related to women's increased commitment to the labor force, which in turn may serve to reduce their poverty in old age. There is convincing evidence of improved mental health at midlife–less depression and increased self-esteem–compared to the 1950s because of women's increased economic independence and self-direction (McGrath, Keita, Strickland, & Russo, 1990). Clearly midlife women are myth-defying in their complexity and in their challenge to slowly changing societal norms about "women's place" and women's capacities.

Of course, women still struggle in a male-dominated society. They deal with sexual harassment, lower wages, glass ceilings, and now glass walls. Two of the most striking characteristics of the United States today is women's increasing poverty and the increasing number of women who are single heads of households (Spain, 1988). Of the population living in poverty, 28 percent of Whites and 61 percent of Blacks live in female-headed households. Impoverished women are a high risk population because they lack supports or resources, experience undue stress, and have reduced access to health services. Despite all this gloom, however, more and more women are defining and determining their own lives. This appears particularly true of midlife women whose creativity and generativity, in Heilbrun's (1988) words, arise from their work and relationships with other women, and not from the "marriage plot" that traditionally defined women's lives. Becoming a "Crone" when one turns 50 may mean becoming pregnant with oneself, at last (LeGuin, 1989).

REFERENCES

Barnett, R.C., Biener, L., & Baruch, G.K. (1987). *Gender and stress.* New York: The Free Press.

Baruch, G.K., Barnett, R.C., & Rivers, C. (1983). *Lifeprints: New patterns of life and work for today's women.* New York: McGraw-Hill.

Baruch, G., & Brooks-Gunn, J. (Eds.) (1984). *Women in midlife.* New York: Plenum.

Bernard, J. (1975). *Women, wives, and mothers.* Chicago, Il: Aldine.

Davis, B.M., & Gilbert, L.A. (1989). Effect of dispositional and situational influences on women's dominance expression in mixed-sex dyads. *Journal of Personality and Social Psychology, 57,* 294-300.

Eckholm, E. (1991, December 1). A tough case for Dr. Healy. *New York Times Magazine,* pp. 67, 68, 122-124.

Fodor, I.G., & Franks, V. (1990). Women at midlife and beyond. *Psychology of Women Quarterly, 14* (4).

Giele, J.Z. (Ed.) (1982). Women's work and family roles. In J.Z. Giele (Ed.), *Women in the middle years* (pp. 115-150). New York: John Wiley.

Gilbert, L.A. (1988). *Sharing it all: The rewards and struggles of two-career families.* New York: Plenum.

Gilbert, L.A. (1992). Gender and counseling psychology: Current knowledge and directions for research and social action. In S.D. Brown & R.W. Lent (Eds.), *Handbook of counseling psychology.*

Gilbert, L.A., & Davidson, S. (1989). Dual-career families at midlife. In S. Hunter & M. Sundel (Eds.), *Midlife myths: Issues, findings, and practice implications* (pp. 195-209). Newbury Park, CA: Sage.

Gilbert, L.A., & Scher, M. (1989). The power of an unconscious belief: Male entitlement and sexual intimacy with clients. *Professional Practice of Psychology, 8,* 94-108.

Hare-Mustin, R.T., & Marecek, J. (1990). *Making a difference: Psychology and the construction of gender.* New Haven: Yale University Press.

Heilbrun, C.G. (1988). *Writing a woman's life.* New York: Balentine Books.

Hunter, S., & Sundel, M. (Eds.) (1989). *Midlife myths: Issues, findings, and practical applications.* Newbury Park, CA: Sage.

LeGuin, U.K. (1989). *Dancing at the edge of the world.* New York: Grove.

Marecek, J. (Ed.). (1989). Theory and method in feminist psychology. *Psychology of Women Quarterly, 13.*

Marecek, J., & Hare-Mustin, R.T. (1991). A short history of the future: Feminism and clinical psychology. *Psychology of Women Quarterly, 15,* 521-536.

McGrath, E., Keita, G.P., Strickland, B., & Russo, N.F. (1990). *Women and depression: Risk factors and treatment issues.* Washington, DC: American Psychological Association.

McHugh, M.C., Koeske, R.D., & Frieze, I.H. (1986). Issues to consider in conducting nonsexist psychology: A review with recommendations. *American Psychologist, 41,* 879-890.

Morrison, A.M., White, R.P., Velsor, E.V., & The Center for Creative Leadership (1987). *Breaking the glass ceiling: Can women reach the top of America's largest corporations?* New York: Addison-Wesley.

National Women's Health Network (1989). *Taking hormones and women's health: Choices, risks, benefits.* (Available from NWHN, 1325 G. Street, N.W., Washington, D.C. 20005.

Neugarten, B.L. (1968). The awareness of middle age. In B.L. Neugarten (Ed.), *Middle age and aging* (pp. 93-98). Chicago: University of Chicago Press.

Rodin, J., & Ickovics, J.R. (1990). Women's health: Review and research agenda as we approach the 21st Century. *American Psychologist, 43*, 1018-1034.

Rossi, A.S. (1980). Life-span theories and women's lives. *Signs: Journal of Women in Culture and Society, 6*, 4-32.

Sherif, C.W. (1982). Needed concepts in the study of gender identity. *Psychology of Women Quarterly, 6*, 375-398.

Spain, D. (1988, November). Women's demographic past, present, and future. Paper presented at the Radcliffe Conference on Women in the 21st Century, Cambridge, MA.

Unger, R.K. (1990). Imperfect reflections of reality. In R. T. Hare-Mustin & J. Marecek (Eds.), *Making a difference: Psychology and the construction of gender.* New Haven: Yale University Press.

United Nations (1991). *The women's world 1970-1990. Trends and statistics.*

Wallston, B.S. (1981). What are the questions in the psychology of women? *Psychology of Women Quarterly, 5*, 597-617.

Westkott, M. (1986). *The feminist legacy of Karen Horney.* New Haven: Yale University Press.

The Significance of the 50th Birthday for Women's Individuation

Pirkko Niemelä
Ritva Lento

SUMMARY. A comparison of 49-51 year old women with 52-55 year old women shows that the older women experience their lives and relations more positively. It seems that they have recently gone through a change in relation to their children, partner, work, and friends. They are less worried about their health and less afraid of illness. They accept death more readily. The results indicate that the women who are a couple of years over 50 have worked through an emotional crisis catalysed by their 50th birthdays.

The emotional crisis is discussed within the framework of female stereotypes. A woman who realizes that she is no longer young is also confronted by the realization that she no longer fits the positive female stereotypes which belong to a young woman in Western culture. This might be an impetus for personal change.

THE 50TH BIRTHDAY

Whether you are a woman or a man, your 50th birthday is especially noted in Finland. Unless you particularly notify the news information center not to do so, they will announce it in the newspapers. Everybody will usually know about this birthday; indeed, in a

Pirkko Niemelä, PhD, is a professor in the Dept. of Psychology, University of Turku, Finland. She has studied at Turku, Uppsala, UCBerkeley, UCLA, and Stockholm, researching the psychological processes and effects of the support systems in women's life turning-points, e.g., becoming a mother, homemother returning to work, abortion, divorce. She became a psychotherapist in 1980, a Family therapist in 1984, and a Psychoanalyst (IPA) in 1989. Ritva Lento, MA, has studied at Turku, and is now working as a clinical psychologist at a mental health clinic in Turku.

small community you are expected to invite everybody to a big party. The only way to avoid the costs of the party, and being the focus of attention for the day, is to travel away and announce this in the newspapers. You simply cannot let this day pass without doing something.

When we started the study of middle-aged women's thoughts and feelings about getting older, we were primarily interested in how women differed from one another and how these differences related to various life-choices. We did not expect the 50th birthday would have any special meaning. Our results, however, made us think again.

THE STUDY

Thirty healthy, white, heterosexual women, ranging in age from 49 to 55 years, ten of them housewives with children, ten working mothers, and ten single working women were randomly selected from within the central district of the city of Turku.

We interviewed each woman individually for about six hours. During these semi-structured interviews, the women spoke of their lives, then answered questions concerning different phases of their lives, their present life-situations, and their expectations for their futures. The questions dealt with work, intimate relationships, and motherhood, as well as free time, interests, and friends. Each woman also talked about how she experienced her health, her age, and the idea of dying. The women's self-perceptions as well as the interviewers' observations were recorded.

In order to check the effects of the age, the women were divided into a younger group and an older group, consisting of 17 women aged 49-51 and 13 women of 52-55 years. The younger group consisted of six single women, five working mothers, and six housewives; the older group had four single women, five working mothers, and four housewives. The groups did not differ in respect to education or vocational status.

Differences between the groups were tested by t-test. In the following the 'risk value for a false conclusion' (p) is given in parentheses. Some results are reported even when the p-value is above .05, and the result is thus not statistically significant. This is done only when these nonsignificant results converge with a statistically significant result giving more information about it.

LIFE IN RETROSPECT

The women in the two groups experience in differing ways the difficulties they have had: younger women talk more about the negative effects of those difficulties, while older ones emphasize their positive consequences (p = .11).

The younger women say that their difficulties have shocked them and that they have not been sufficiently prepared (p = .02). The older women report more often that the difficult periods of their lives have turned into positive experiences (p = .12).

What the women say about their lives does not indicate that the younger women's lives have actually been more difficult. Rather, the real difference is in the way the women now take their difficulties; even where there is no difference in the number of 'life changes' between the two groups, the younger ones experience their changes more negatively (p = .03). They seem to be at the beginning of the working-through process and therefore experience their lives as harder. From their mid-crisis perspective, the period leading to it–even their youth–is seen in darker hues (p = .12). The older women have had more time to work through their difficulties, hence are able to see them with the benefit of several points of view. The interviewers rated that the older women were more interested in discussing and 'pondering on' their lives (p = .11).

PERSONAL SUPPORT

When discussing the idea of support during their difficulties, the younger women talk more about support from their own children (p = .10) as well as from parents and siblings (p = .05). The real difference is probably not in the amount of support, but in the present experience of the women. The older women are at the stage where they feel they have 'cleared out' their difficulties and have themselves changed by going through this process.

THE PRESENT AND THE FUTURE

There are differences between the two groups in regard to the number of conflicts in the present life-situation. However, according to the interviewers' ratings, the younger women also experience their present life-situation as more difficult (p = .03), the older women more often feeling they will cope with clearing out their difficulties (p = .04).

There are no differences in how the two groups perceive their personal futures; the amount of time remaining to them, and its threats, are perceived similarly. The women as a whole do not see the future any more as a time when their own wishes and plans will be realized. The older women have accepted the lack of expected positive life-changes (p = .003), saying, for example, "life is just like it is," "I have to be satisfied with what I have," and "I can't do anything about it." Still, the older women are somewhat more optimistic about the development of their community, and the world at large (p = .11).

What do these women think when they think of their futures? There are no differences in how much they worry about their partners, children, or work. The difference is that the younger women think more about their intimate relationships (p = .04), while the older ones think more about death (p = .12).

MARRIAGE

Among the married women, the younger ones are more likely to feel the marital relationship has recently worsened, while the older ones are likely to see it as having taken a turn for the better (p = .05). According to the interviewer's ratings, the younger women's marital relationships are more conflict-ridden (p = .13), and they feel they have less influence on decisions made at home (p = .04). The younger women feel they have become more distant from their husbands (p = .03) and their husbands from them (p = .02). The older women are more ready to invest themselves in the marital relationship (p = .04).

Most of the women are in the marital phase in which their children have just left, or are preparing to leave, home. The younger women do not yet accept this phase as readily as the older ones (p = .02).

MOTHERHOOD

The younger women still have more children at home (p = .05). There is no difference between the two groups in the age of the women's older children, but the younger mothers' youngest child is, on average, 18.0 years, where the older mothers' youngest child averages 23.8 years (p = .05).

The older women experience their children as having become more distant from them (p = .03) and feel their relationship with their children has become a more equal one (p = .000). These women have also discussed more with other people their children's increasing independence (p = .01).

According to the interviewer's ratings, the younger women are more stuck in their mother-role (p = .02), more tied to their children (p = .003), and more in need of their children (p = .01). These ratings suggest the older women have come further in the process of changing their relationship with their becoming-independent children (p = .06). Further, this process has raised these mothers' self-esteem (p = .02).

WORK AND LEISURE

There is no difference between the groups in vocational-choice satisfaction, though the older women accept more what they have achieved in their work (p = .08). However, they speak more often of an earlier experience of loss upon realizing they will never attain their vocational goals (p = .11). It seems that the older women have been able to mourn what they have failed to attain, so they can now be satisfied with their work.

The younger women have more interests and hobbies outside home (p = .12) and the number of things in which they are interested has increased recently (p = .06). The younger women are more interested in their hobbies (p = .003) and intend to have more free time for themselves (p = .08). The older women emphasize less their need for personal free time (p = .08) and are moderately satisfied with how they use the free time they have. The younger women are more satisfied with their use of their free time (p = .03) and experience it as more important (p = .04) than do the older women. Conversely, this latter group are more interested in social development and world events (p = .05).

The younger women seem to be in a life-phase in which they are reaching out from the home; the older women, seeming to have experienced this phase, are now coordinating their time with their family members.

FRIENDSHIPS

The older women have recently developed more new friendships than have the younger women (p = .003). However, there is no difference in the quality or differentiality of the two groups' friendship-relationships. The interviewers estimate the older women to have a greater wish to be independent in such relationships (p = .08).

HEALTH AND AGING

There are women with menopausal symptoms in both age groups. The older women accept their menopause better (p = .04) and have come further in this physiological process. The younger women are more likely than the older ones to feel that their health has deteriorated (p = .09), are more afraid of illness (p = .08), and experience more dizziness (p = .12) and sleeping difficulties (p = .05). They are also more depressed, both according to their own report (p = .09) and according to the interviewer's ratings (p = .045). The younger women seem more unhappy with consequences both for their mental and their somatic health.

There are no differences between the age groups in the worries and threats they associate with aging. Still, the older women accept that they are getting older, denying less the difficulties associated with aging (p = .08) and isolating less their own feelings about it (p =

.09). Also attitudes toward death differ for the two groups: the older women are more able to think of death as an end to their own lives (p = .10).

OTHER STUDIES

There are other comparative studies of younger and older middle aged women: Ursula Lehr's (1961) comparison of 40-49 year-old women with a group over 50 years, and Lowenthal, Thurnher and Chiriboga's (1975) comparison of a group of women whose average age was 48 with a group who averaged 58, both describe many similar differences to those detailed here.

According to these studies, the younger women were more pessimistic about life-changes. In Lehr's study, they were more afraid of getting old and more worried about losing their attractiveness than were the older women, who accepted death better and were more able to integrate ideas of it into their thoughts of the future.

According to Lehr's study, older women were more satisfied with their human relationships and more independent. The younger women experienced their marriages more negatively and as more full of conflicts. Lowenthal et al., (1975) reported the younger women of their study to be more concerned for their marriages and more dependent upon their husbands. Further, these women centered more on their families and focused their wishes on their children.

Taken together, these three studies seem to describe the effects of the same working-through processes. However, the age-difference in the earlier studies was much larger; it is surprising that these effects can be described by comparing women who are 49-51 years old with those of 52-55 years.

IMPETUS FOR CHANGE?

What can affect this rapid change? In this study, the youngest of the older women's children were some years older than those of the younger women. Could the age of this youngest child, and his/her attendant processes of becoming independent, be so crucial to a mother's development?

In many studies, the senior author has been interested in the mother-image and the 'ideal mother' stereotype (e.g., Niemelä, 1982). In studies describing changes in the ways mothers experience themselves as mothers, she shows that these changes are gradual. For example, many women whose children are already of school age still wish to have the role of a small child's mother and change their role very slowly (Niemelä, 1981). Given this gradual nature of role change, even if its impetus–the youngest child becoming independent–is of great importance, we think the sudden change we have noted in the present study cannot be understood in terms of it, particularly as a third of the women questioned had no children.

WHAT THE WOMEN SAID

Following these unexpected results–of many differences between close and ostensibly similar age groups–we returned to the interviews and looked for explanations in what the women themselves said.

Many talked of the effect of the 50th birthday with regard to the process of accepting aging. Several women explicitly stated that it was this day that made them think they were getting old, even if the interviewer did not ask about it in particular.

One said: "The first time I thought that I was going to be old was on my 50th birthday. It was my birthday that made me think so. It struck me in the morning. It was awful." And another: "My colleagues said they would come to me for my 50th birthday. I thought, 'When I was young I used to think that a person who was 50 was old.' It came to me so suddenly. It felt cold and gloomy."

Their 50th birthdays shook these women up, starting a process of rethinking and re-evaluation of their entire lives.

SELF IMAGE

Perhaps the most important part of the re-evaluation process, the change of the women's images of themselves, starts by their realizing they are no longer young.

All the positive stereotypes of women in our culture are of young women. The 'ideal woman' is an attractive sex-object, a giving, self-sacrificing mother, or an attractive and effective career-woman. Most women are very aware of these stereotypes, and as long as they perceive of themselves as young, try to fit their expectations.

When a woman realizes she is no longer young, she realizes, too, that she can no longer fit these stereotypes. For most people, it is painful to become aware of increasing age, of illness, and of death. It is also difficult to come to terms with the idea that one can no longer be 'feminine' in the way we women have thought we should be.

FINDING ONESELF

But when we cannot any longer aspire to be what we feel others expect us to be, what can we do? We can start by thinking about who we really are, by getting more in with our real feelings and thoughts, our needs and wishes, and our role in fulfilling them. Through abandoning the possibilities of realizing others' expectations of how we should be, we can get in touch with ourselves.

BITTERNESS

Younger women in this study said "I am bitter," "My difficulties have left bitterness in me," "the fights are in my thoughts." This bitterness leads to distancing from others: "I have become restless, and colder to others," "I don't want to discuss things because it doesn't help," "I've lost my trust in others." These women do not feel they are in control of their lives. Instead, they feel dependent on others, and that those 'others' are not fulfilling their expectations.

INDEPENDENCE

Older women express more independence. They are now in the center of their own lives and feel responsible for them. They have achieved more contact with themselves, know better who they are and what they want. They have reevaluated their needs: "I have started evaluating other things–instead of the material, I have started valuing health and small joys." They feel more able to influence the events and the course of their own lives: "I want to clear up the difficulties." They feel in contact with themselves: "I have learned to know me better."

When one can accept oneself, and feel in control of one's own life, one can also accept others better: "I've started to think in a new way, to understand others better, and my world has become bigger," "Now I understand my own parents better," "Now I see the positive sides of my husband."

SEPARATION-INDIVIDUATION

Margaret Mahler, Fred Pine, and Anne Bergman (1975) have described how a small child separates gradually from her mother and starts becoming an individual. This separation-individuation process continues throughout one's life, with 'turning points' in life serving as impetuses to it. In coming into contact with their own feelings and needs, the older women in this study have taken one more step in this process, becoming independent from their husbands, children, and close friends, and becoming able to forge more equal relationships with others.

An important aspect of woman's individuation is therefore becoming her own focus, defining herself by her own concepts and experiences. It seems that the 50th birthday makes many Finnish women begin this process of self-focused individuation.

BIRTHDAY MAGIC?

How can a birthday, a wholly artificial, arbitrary boundary, be so important? Are the developmental changes associated with age?

Earlier developmental psychologists emphasized the significance of the midlife crisis. Pearlin (1975) and Baruch (1984) challenge this view, emphasizing that the age itself does not create the crisis. However, Daniel Levinson et al. (1978) has demonstrated age-related transitional periods in men's lives, and the age thus seems to matter. But how does the age bring about the developmental changes?

The results of the present study relate developmental changes to age, but the developments that occur at 50 are not understood as functions of age per se, but of the women's knowledge of being 50.

REFERENCES

Baruch, G.K. (1984). The psychological well-being of women in the middle years. In G. Baruch & J. Brooks-Gunn (Eds.), *Women in Midlife.* New York and London: Plenum Press.

Lehr. (1961). Veränderung der daseinsthematik der frau im erwachsenenalter. *Vita humana,* 4, 193-228.

Levinson, D., Darrow, C., Klein, E., Levinson, M. & McKee, B. (1978). *The seasons of a man's life.* New York: Alfred A. Knopf.

Lowenhal, M.F., Thurnher, M. & Chiriboga, D. (1975) *Four stages of life: a comparative study of women and men facing transition.* San Francisco: Jossey-Bass.

Niemelä, P. (1981). The housewife's process of identity change in cognition, emotion and action. *International council of psychologists congress,* Los Angeles.

Niemelä, P. (1982). Overemphasis of mother role and the inflexibility of roles. In I. Gross, J. Downing, & A. d'Heurle (Eds.), *Sex role attitudes and cultural change.* Boston: D. Reidel Publishing Company.

Mahler, M.S., Pine, F. and Bergman, A. (1975). *The psychological birth of the human infant.* New York: Basic Books.

Pearlin, L. (1975). Sex roles and depression. In N. Datan & L.H. Ginsberg (Eds.) *Life span developmental psychology: normative life crises.* New York: Academic Press.

Older Never Married Women: A Cross-Cultural Investigation

Sharyn A. Paradise

SUMMARY. A U.S. Department of Health, Education and Welfare report (Peace, 1981) and a United Nations source (Haney, 1980), emphatically identify that by the year 2000 the single most important fact in an aging society is that it will be primarily female; more than half of these women will live singly. The purpose of this research is to examine the life themes and coping skills of older never married women. It is hoped that the results of this research will move us away from stereotypes into a broader and more encompassing view of this group. The implications for redesign of an infrastructure which supports older women's needs is discussed.

INTRODUCTION

This study investigates the normative values and stereotypes of never married women and its implications for the redesign of an infrastructure which supports them. Attitudes and behaviors, particularly those culled from family research on caucasian middle class couples and nuclear families, have become standards of the definition of "family" in North American society. Even in the age of increased awareness of racial, ethnic, sexual preference, and global differences in family models, the standards set by this prior research linger on. At best, minority groups are negatively stereotyped as deviant or socially problematic, at best. This study examines the central themes in women's lives as they progress to older adulthood: the similarities and misnomers.

Sharyn A. Paradise, PhD, is a counselor educator at New Mexico Highlands University and a cross cultural researcher/trainer in the area of older women's issues in developing countries.

One must note, however, that traditional family research also focuses on the course of women's lives as defined by societal expectations that women sequence their lives according to rites of passage such as marriage and parenting (Rossi, 1980). These rites of passage are commonly acknowledged in couples and nuclear families but not in the lives of older never married women. One of the questions raised in Katherine Allen's (1989) research addressed similarities of theme in older never married women's lives, utilizing a qualitative life history research model. Allen (1989) focused her research however on caucasian "blue collar" women. She provided some important insights into the family dynamics regarding separation, individuation, and kin-keeping roles of the unmarried women in these families, but more importantly, she established the participatory research design used in this study.

The research process was initiated through a snowball technique (Bogdan and Biklen, 1982). The researcher contacted U.S. based agencies and U.S Peace Corps projects working with older women in Jamaica. Initial contact was made with potential participants identified by the agencies involved, who were also asked for names of other women in similar circumstances. Participants were selected from both urban and rural areas; no attempt was made to match women to socioeconomic or educational levels, although the effects of the cohort (born between 1920 and 1940) will be discussed as part of the time, context, and process structure experienced by these individuals and families.

Of the initial 20 women interviewed, six were chosen, three women from the United States and three from Jamaica. An open ended interview was used to establish initial rapport and eligibility for the study. Several descriptive questions were asked to establish place in the cohort and never married status for eligibility in the study. A second more in depth but less structured interview was conducted with a series of open ended questions regarding demographics, genogram construction, life events, family relationships, and kin-keeping roles. The participants were asked for permission to video and audio tape.

However, no attempt was made to select participants on the basis of income, given the inherent difficulties of gathering such information from older women living in different cultures.

Data was collected from the interview forms and transcriptions of the actual taped interviews. The researcher then coded the data and searched for common themes and differences. The focus for analysis of the data was at three levels of generality: the search for universals across the experiences (what seemed true for all the women); group differences due to race, class and culture (what seems true for the groups within the sample); and individual characteristics. Representative quotations were used to illustrate some of the universal themes.

DISCUSSION

The cohort group of six women were born between 1920 and 1940. Four women came from two-parent families while the other two were raised by single parents. Five of the women in the study reported themselves to be first born children in the family. The additional member of the study was an only child. The birth order results reflected similar findings in Allen's (1989) study. Three women were from middle class homes while the others placed themselves in a low socioeconomic class. Four of the women in the study still lived in the family home at the time of the interview while the other two lived within a 30 miles radius of a parent.

The Jamaican women attended "All Age School," a government school. The required tuition was usually paid by the father. Two women were not allowed to complete school, the third Jamaican stopped out for 20 years and returned to a technical school to complete her education. A typical Jamaican women shared this:

I went to a government school. My father wanted me to drop out, and he wouldn't pay the tuition because the oldest girl in the family doesn't go to school. Then my father found out I was talking to a brown skinned boy (my father thought he would make me pregnant).

My father got drunk and beat me up with a bicycle pump. He said I could not go to school after that. I grew up with my grandmother soon after that and she sent me to learn sewing.

All of the U.S. women completed high school without reported barriers; one went on to complete graduate work at the Master's level. The occupations of the U.S. women included a machinist, bookkeeper, and teacher. The U.S. women reported the following:

There was no problem, I was always expected to go to college and teach. I did what I was told and it was near my mother! I never really left home.

School was good but I always said I was married to Mr. Sears (Sears and Roebuck was her employer) *for 35 years. I loved being a bookkeeper, until the end when I had to decide to travel with the company or caretake my father. I did both with help.*

I was a machinist for several years during the war (World War II) *but I had to return home. My mother was alone at the time. My sister married and I came home to stay with mom.*

The Jamaican women worked as a street vendor (higgler), nurse aide, and a small business owner. They reported similar results which reflected a conflict between family and external jobs.

Two of the Jamaican women reported an occupational progression beginning with seamstress work and farming to upwardly mobile professions: small business owner and nurses aide:

My family had a little land in the bush. After a while I returned to the village to start my own business. My sister's kids were like mine and then she moved away. I chose to go to nursing school then but never finished.

It was quite clear that the both the U.S. and Jamaican women the cross-cultural sample reflected kin-keeping as a primary criterion for choosing a compatible job outside the home.

LOSS OF PARENT(S): JAMAICAN SAMPLE

Miss Ivey is a woman who is a higgler (street vendor) in the ghetto of Kingston, Jamaica. She was 44 years old when her father died.

I've learned to take care of myself and home. The politicals killed him. We lost our house as well. I have had a hard life: higglering on the streets. I still take care of my mother. She is in poor health.

Miss Dorothy is a small business woman who owns her own "Social Club" where Portland residents play dominoes and drink rum. Miss Dorothy's mother died when she was 30 years old and she was still working on the family plantation in the bush.

I've learned to take care of myself, you know. I take care of the neighborhood kids, now. I miss her very much. When she died I started this business.

Miss Cathryn, a nurses aide in Kingston Jamaica, reported both her parents as "alive and well": *When my mother gets sick, of course, I will take care of her. It is my job, you see. She is family even when she hates me.*

U.S. SAMPLE

Frances worked the majority of her life as a machinist in factories nearby her parents' home. She was 18 years old when her father died and 30 years old when her mother died.

I had to take care of my mother when my dad died in the mines. I changed jobs to be closer to her. When she died, I still had my brother's kids to take care of . . . he drank!

Susan worked for Sears Roebuck and loved her career. She was 36 years old when her mother died of a long terminal illness and her dad's illness lasted for the next 14 years. She became so involved in the caretaking of her parents that she became an advocate for better nursing care when she retired at age 55.

I killed her (my mother) . . . I pulled her I.V. and lied to her about it. There was "no hope" the doctor said. The I.V. ran out and I said goodbye. I returned to work after this, and my dad lived with me.

Alice, now a college teacher, lost her father when she was 50 years old and her mother five years later. Both her parents lived with her until they died.

When my dad died suddenly, I worked and took care of my mother. I was relieved when she died. I just kept working at school, even more afraid of being alone.

One notes a trend in responses to the death of a parent in life, a transference of caretaking role to the next parent. In addition, caretaking predictably focused on siblings and neighborhood children. The one interesting exception in form of caretaking role was the development of a retirement "job" as an advocate for better health care in nursing homes(U.S. participant): "I want to be sure that when I need a nursing home, it will be there for me."

These results echo a traditional 19th and 20th century familistic ideology which implies that one keeps the family of origin intact at any cost and that when the family of origin ceases, the tradition moves to maintaining the extended family. The effect of such ideology on these women was a conflict between individual needs and family demands. Feelings of anger, frustration, and guilt were commonly reported.

The processes by which these women decided not to marry is really a culmination of a series of life events related to friends, family, education, and work. When asked about why they did not marry, the women in the U.S. sample made the following statements:

I always said I was married to Mr. Sears (job) *for 35 years. I never wanted to marry.*

My mother needed me. My father died and there was no time to marry. I could not leave her!

The Jamaican responses were quite reflective of a West Indian cultural milieu of marriage/misogyny:

Man would beat me up and I wouldn't take it because I am a mere [means "powerful" in Patois language] *woman. I am strong and feisty (independent). I buck up against men that are wild and who want to use me. I'm smart. Me . . I feel dem out. A primary relationship should be good but it is not; men running around wid alcohol and such!*

PERSPECTIVES ON WORK

The U.S. women reported higher degrees of satisfaction on the job outside the home than their Jamaican counterparts. The two women who reported job satisfaction in the U.S sample and the one in the Jamaican sample also had higher levels of education and income.

Some women spoke of a struggle to maintain individual identity while balancing kin-keeping (parental caregiving) with work outside the home. The majority of the women described parental caregiving as a life long course. In fact, the first born women reported interdependent careers (family and outside job) in all instances. They also commented on the defined job of kinkeeping:

Serving gives me satisfaction; it is the purpose of life and keeps me going, but I don't always like it.

The women in the U.S. sample reflected on the availability of respite care. Many of them said it was better to keep working and have someone come into the house and take care of the parent. Such resources, however, were not available in the developing world of Jamaica, West Indies.

Many of the Jamaican women were socially conditioned as early as age 11 to be kin-keepers:

My mother was an only girl. She lacked direction and insight to change, so I took care of her when I was 11. The hurricanes came and I was sent to take care of my grandmother and her brother. I took care of my grandmother until she died thirty-five years later. I got offers to go abroad but I would not leave my grandmother. You know. It wasn't bad. I wanted to go to nursing school but then my mother hurt her foot in an accident and I couldn't leave them both. My brother left, but I couldn't.

Many of the women in the sample voiced feelings of ambivalence, anger, and guilt regarding care-taking issues. Yet, they also reported feelings of intimacy and mutuality similar to those experienced by married women. This affirms the belief that women do not have to marry to form bonded relationships. In fact, the literature (Rubin,1983) demonstrates that many women seek intimacy from friends outside marriage anyway.

All of the women in the study had been involved with children, to varying degrees. The Jamaican women tended to be more involved as surrogate mothers to extended family members. Miss Ivey lived in the Kingston Jamaica ghetto. She had chosen to have children without a husband; "The child give me more meaning to life . . . someone to take care of me when I am old!"

The role of surrogate care taking of a sibling's children is also reported in Allen's (1989) study. Allen (1989) noted that the move to care-take sibling's children was associated with a shift to a matriarchal family structure which focused on the never married woman as head of the family. This could account for the patterns in Jamaican women who were born years before the patriarchal shift (1940's) took place in the West Indies.

The U.S. women reported some ambivalence about not having children: "I think I would have liked to have had a child, myself. But then, I wonder, why bother!" When asked if life would have been different if they had married and had children, many of them said "yes" to the difference but "not necessarily better."

The Jamaican responses were a bit different perhaps because although there is some formal marriage in the Catholic communities of the capital city, there is none in the ghettos or the "bush" country. Hence this was a difficult question for many of the Jamaican women to respond to, as many of them could not marry or did not want to marry because of the norm of battering. Miss Ivey said: "I don't know if marriage would be successful for me because men should not beat women and they are tricky in the brain."

The majority of women in both groups supported a healthy outlook about singlehood. They indicated that they had no regrets about not marrying, and in many cases, preferred to be single. Susan stated that she regretted not marrying or having children, but went on to qualify her regrets by talking about surrogate parenting of her sister's children and having a career too.

When asked what was the highest/happiest time of life, the U.S. women typically responded:

The highest point for me was my retirement party when I found out I had so many friends. It was a memorable day. I knew what a good job I had done!

The Jamaican women represented a different view of the highest/ happiest time of life:

I am most happy when I am "sportin" [socializing]. I dress up and go down by de road and listen to de music and talk to intelligent people.

My highest point is when my brother from abroad (England) sends me postcards and says he'll help me when I get old.

Predictably, the U.S. sample focused on outside career and the ritual of retirement as recognition of a job well done. The Jamaican women were not part of an industrialized society and, for the most part, were reared in a matriarchal society which was shifting to patriarchy at the time when they were middle aged adults. The values of upward mobility through education seemed of great importance to the Jamaican women.

When further questioned about how each planned to spend time after the age of working outside or within the home, the U.S. women stated:

It was my goal to retire. I planned for it so I would be secure and be able to travel. I am doing volunteer work to keep busy. My health is not bad so I can get around well. I will stay in this house, it was my parents and now it is mine.

The Jamaican women stated:

I will stay here in the house my family left me. I'll improve on it. My health is not so good and I cannot work anymore. Who will take care of me when I need it? I am worried.

The U.S. sample differed from the Jamaican sample, as expected. Many of the U.S. women knew how to plan for retirement, a strength of single never married women living in Western society.

Women from developing countries face the dilemmas of limited access health care and the tradition of familial caretaking as a retirement plan. The system is breaking down as Western industry and urban living arrive in Jamaica. Women are forced to leave the villages and the "bush" to go to the city for health care; this is a phenomenon which forces them even further, geographically, from their neighborhoods and potential caretakers.

In order to cope with aging, the literature (Allen, 1989) speaks to the issues of never married women being adept at forming "a community of friends" as support. Statements from both U.S. and Jamaican women corroborate this coping skill.

We're good friends, you know. I had this cold and flu, last Tuesday and she called to make sure I was alright. She was worried about my well being and I am worried about hers. We care.

One of the ways to cope with the financial and emotional realities of being older is to bond with other women in similar positions. Both the U.S. and Jamaican women voiced their desires to become part of a community of friends as they progressed through the later stages of life. The community of friends seemed the best alternative to loneliness, intimacy, and caretaking needs, say these women.

CONCLUSION

While it is true never married women have tended to be traditionally viewed as deviant" old "maids and lesbians or women who couldn't get a man" (Rossi, 1980), the data suggests that this view is in fact incorrect. All the women in this study reported high levels of functioning and satisfaction in their lives.

The Jamaican women came from a matriarchal legacy. Their roles changed when British patriarchy (1940's) entered the culture and women were de-valued, a phenomenon not uncommon to women in western cultures. Only one of the women in the Jamaican sample was born during patriarchy. The other two reflect the strong values of matriarchal transmission of values, culture, teaching, nurturing, and cooperation.

The U.S. women reflected attitudes similar to the Jamaican woman born during 1940; they acknowledged the de-valuing of the caretaking role and a desire to be upwardly mobile through careers outside the home.

All women were connected to their families and learned a familistic ideology which dictates coordination of life and career decisions with family needs. All of the women in this study had at least one intimate connection to another adult member of the family and shared the experience of mothering in various perspectives. All worked outside the home during their adult lives, yet remained unacknowledged for the invisible work they did as caretakers. All the women lived with parents for some time during their lives and were able to work out the issues of the parent/child symbiosis, individuation, and separation by middle age. The opportunity to resolve family conflicts was enhanced by geographical proximity.

Their stories reinforced the power of family socialization and social expectations that women marry and have children. Yet the majority reported very active and fulfilling lives.

In the year 2000, more than half the world will be elderly women, many of these women will be left widowed and or will have chosen to remain single. Much can be learned from the lives of single women to help in this transition. One must begin to view the world through a "female lens" (Rhodes, 1983). As societies develop, more women will be affected negatively by rapid industrialization and institutional models of care for the elderly. Other models for care will be needed on an international scale.

Lastly, one must research and teach and expand the normative of family lifestyles to include an array of alternatives, one of which is to remain single and quite well adjusted!

REFERENCES

Allen, K.(1989). *Single women/family ties.* London: Sage.
Bogdan, R. & Biklen, S. (1982). *Qualitative research for education.* Boston: Allyn and Bacon.
Haney, J. (1980). *Workshop on the growing older female.* Maryland: University of Maryland Press.
Peace, S. (1981). *An international perspective on the status of the older woman.* Washington, D.C.: International Federation of Aging.
Rhodes, L. (1983). *Aging and women's status.* Barbados: U.N. NGO Committee Report on Aging.
Rossi, A. (1980). Life span theories of women's lives. *Signs: International Women in Culture and Society,* 6, 4-32.
Rubin, L. (1983) Intimate strangers: Men and women together. N.Y.: Harper *Colophon.*

Older Women Coping with Divorce:
Peer Support Groups

Carol Wechsler Blatter
Jamia Jasper Jacobsen

SUMMARY. This paper identifies mid and later life divorce as a life cycle crisis and phase of transformation experienced by an increasing number of older heterosexual women. As women live longer, projections suggest that increasing numbers will divorce in their later years. Despite these trends, there is a lack of research and suggested treatment strategies.

Since divorce has serious negative economic and social consequences for older heterosexual women, helping them to cope with this crisis is an important mental health challenge. This paper describes the peer support group model program, "Expanding Horizons," which enables women to heal and reconnect with others through participation and sharing with peers. This psychotherapist-facilitated service is affordable, accessible, and relevant.

Another challenge addressed in this paper is helping the adult children of recently divorced parents. There is little known about the impact of parental divorce on adult children. However, there is a tendency for divorce to be repeated in successive generations. Research suggests that young women, more than men, have emotional difficulty with parental divorce. The authors are suggesting intergenerational work with peer support groups for recently divorced mothers and their young adult daughters. This intervention may contribute to intergenerational family stability.

Carol Wechsler Blatter, MSW, ACSW, BCD, is a clinical social worker, marriage and family therapist, consultant, and trainer in private practice, specializing in aging and marital/family issues. She has published articles on aging, divorce, and geriatric case management. Jamia Jasper Jacobsen, PhD, is an individual and family therapist in a medical practice. She is a nationally known speaker and author/editor of three books and has numerous publications to her credit.

INTRODUCTION

Divorce and its concomitant problems have received consider-
able attention. While lack of attention to divorce among older heterosexual people may have been justified in the past by their very
small numbers, there are several trends which indicate divorce will
become an increasingly important issue in mid and later life adjustment. The trends which suggest mid and later life divorce include
societal and individual acceptance of divorce, changing population
trends, and shifting roles of women from home centeredness to
activities outside the home.

Despite these trends and changing demographics, relatively little
attention has been paid to the adjustment of heterosexual women
who divorce in the middle and later adult years. Most of these
women need help coping with an often unanticipated life transition,
while managing other issues typically associated with aging. Life
cycle tasks facing aging women who divorce may include transitioning from the role of wife to the role of a single person, rethinking their identity apart from the one defined by the male spouse,
reworking gender related roles and dependency issues, making
peace with the finality of the childbearing years, developing new
relationships and opportunities which provide esteem building, re-
focusing esteem primarily derived from parenting, accepting adult
children as separate individuals with their own lives, acquiring new
skills for the job market, continuing prior work, planning for retirement, adjusting to grandparenting and, in some cases, part-time or
full-time parenting of grandchildren, parenting their parents, dealing with the pain of increasing losses of family members and
friends, seeing themselves as members of the oldest generation,
managing problems related to physical and mental health, and recognizing increasingly the limits of time and their own mortality.

In the middle and later years of the couple's life cycle, they may
experience renewed closeness, especially as the children leave
home and they re-focus on one another. Women who are divorced at
this time may not experience this renewal. Instead, they may spend
the rest of their lives without mates and without the opportunity for
a shared generativity review, many without financial and emotional
security, and without the societal rights and privileges associated

with widowhood. It is not surprising that several women have told these authors that it would have been much easier if their spouses had died.

As we age, we learn to accept many losses–the loss of our youth which will never be regained, the loss of physical and, in some cases, mental capacity, the loss of control over our lives, the successive losses of family members and friends, and the loss of one's standard of living. Divorce in mid and later life is yet another very serious loss for both men and women. However, women, even more so than men, have difficulty with separation and isolation.

> Whereas separation, differentiation, and autonomy have been considered primary factors in male development, the values of caring and attachment, interdependence, relationship and attention to context have been primary in female development . . . Women have tended to define themselves in the context of human relationships and to judge themselves in terms of their ability to care. (Carter & McGoldrick, 1989, p. 32)

Women have long known the importance of intimacy, affiliation, and caring. The healthy development of women has been thought to lie in their recognition of the continuing importance of attachment in the human life cycle. Given that women are especially vulnerable to problems regarding separation, it is not surprising that an unexpected divorce in mid and later life is experienced as devastating. Based upon the work of Miller (1976), Carter and McGoldrick (1989) state: "The threat of disruption of a relationship is often perceived not just as object loss, but as something closer to one's identity and thus as requiring a transformation of self and of the system" (p. 34). When divorce occurs, older womens' images of themselves must also be transformed. Most women need help with this transformation process, including managing anger and feelings of rejection; developing self-esteem; finding satisfying outside work for economic support and self-growth; creating new patterns and directions which give meaning to their lives as single persons; and reconnecting in new ways with family members. These women must also do what they naturally know how to do, and that is to make connections, develop attachments, and build intimate relationships with others, especially with peers. Because women naturally express their identities through attachment, relationship, and caring, it is important that services be provided which maximize opportunities for building relationships, bonding with others, offering mutual support and nurturance. Hagestad and Smyer (1982) confirm womens' ability to seek out support in this divorce transition period:

> . . . the availability of transitional time becomes critical, especially in cases where the initial movement towards marital dissolution was not started by the individual. It appears from our sample that women, more than men, are able to take charge of such a process, to create lee-time, and to seek out transitional support, particularly in cases when the dissolution was not originally sought by them. (p. 187)

We believe that peer support groups provide the opportunity for help and support during this critical transitional time in the divorce process. These groups provide a therapeutic service which offer peer contacts, networking, and esteem building, while being affordable and easily accessible for most participants.

While both sexes can benefit from participation in peer support groups, women are more likely to avail themselves of the services. Common issues women can deal with include loss, grief, and lowered self-esteem (Rae, Jacobsen, & Blatter, 1991; Schaie & Geiwitz, 1982). Both sexes may be extremely vulnerable and find themselves isolated and disconnected from a support system (McGoldrick, 1989; Rae, Jacobsen, & Blatter, 1991; Silverstein, 1988; Stern Peck, & Manocherian, 1989). Both older men and women face other common problems which include hostility and bitterness from their children, lack of a clear sense of identity, lack of meaning in life, loneliness, lack of emotional support, and sense of isolation (Rae, Jacobsen, & Blatter, 1991; Stern Peck, & Manocherian, 1989). The older spouse who has been left likely feels shame, humiliation, isolation, and lack of desire for new relationships (Stern Peck, & Manocherian, 1989). When their former spouses remarry, they are especially likely to feel abandoned (Ahrons & Rodgers, 1987).

STATISTICS

The divorce rate among older persons has increased. In 1985, 20% of those persons who were married fifteen years or more and were on the average age 56 or more, were divorcing. This is a rise from 4% in 1960, (Gander, 1991; Weitzman, 1985). Otten (1989) cited Uhlenberg and associates who noted that the divorce rate for women doubled between 1960 and 1985 for women in their 40s and increased by 60% for women over 50. "Divorce after midlife, they state, is no longer a rare event . . ." (p. B1). Mid to late life divorce has been estimated to account for 25% of all divorces (Deckert & Langelier, 1978; Rae, Jacobsen, & Blatter, 1991; Uhlenberg, Cooney, & Boyd, 1990). This rate is predicted to increase (DeShane & Brown-Wilson, 1981; Uhlenberg & Myers, 1981).

Gander (1991) refers to Uhlenberg and Myers' (1981) prediction that the divorce rate for persons over the age of 45 will either double or triple over the next 40 years. Between the years 2010 and 2014, one-third of people who reach age 65 will be divorced during their lifetime.

According to United States Bureau of the Census, 1990, the divorce rate for women 50-54 years old is 7.7 per 1000 and for men 10.9 per 1,000. The divorce rate for women 55-59 years old is 4.2 per 1,000 and for men 6.4 per 1,000. The divorce rate for women 60-64 is 2.8 per 1,000 and for men 4.2 per 1,000. Finally, the divorce rate for women 65 and over is 1.5 per 1,000 and for men 2.0 per 1,000.

Gander noted that the current divorce rate does appear to be stabilizing at 4.8 per 1,000 persons as compared to 5.3 per 1,000 in 1979 and 1981. However, the demographics of divorced populations are changing. In 1977, the U.S. Bureau of the Census reported that approximately 600,00 persons over the age of 65 were divorced; by 1979, this figure had increased to 767,000 persons. While all of the increases cannot be attributed to older age divorce, these increases suggest that divorce will become a more important issue in late life adjustment. The long term implication of the demographic shifts among the divorced affect families of all ages. However, research and the literature concerning older and younger divorced persons are few (Gander, 1991; Longfellow, 1991).

REVIEW OF RELATED LITERATURE

As noted, few studies focus on late-life divorce in females. Often the divorced woman has been left by her husband for a younger woman (Silverstein, 1988). When the woman initiates divorce proceedings, she usually has struggled with a long, unhappy marriage (Silverstein, 1988).

Recent studies have compared the effects of divorce on older and younger persons. Some have associated more emotional difficulties with older divorced persons when compared with their younger counterparts. Other results suggest that adverse effects from divorce may not be uniform for women across all age groups (Longfellow, 1991).

> . . . Kitson (1988) scrutinized specific age groupings, confirmation that older persons were the most negatively affected by divorce was lacking. Instead Kitson found that those younger women between 35 and 50 years of age were the most distressed following divorce. (Gander, 1991, p. 177)

Research by Gander focused on post-divorce adjustment factors of older and younger groups of divorced persons. "Data collected from personal interviews indicate that older divorced persons are not devastated by their divorce" (Gander, 1991, p. 175). A predictor of well being for the older group was family closeness.

Uhlenberg and Myers (1981) found that being divorced or separated is "detrimental to one's social and economic welfare in old age" (p. 176). Uhlenberg compared the 1985 economic status of women who were divorced, widowed, and married:

> Divorcees, whether recent or longer-term, were less likely to own their own home than married women or widows, more likely to have to share living arrangements with someone else, more likely to feel obliged to work and generally less well off financially . . . Both widowhood and divorce are economically damaging for older women . . . but "the effects of divorce are generally more severe." (Otten, 1989, p. B1)

Among women who divorce, those who earn higher salaries tend to divorce more frequently than women earning lower salaries. For women, the issues of financial support and the development of skills for the work world are significant (McGoldrick, 1989; Rae, Jacobsen, & Blatter, 1991). Since many women have had disrupted work histories due to raising children, they are more likely to have difficulties finding work and earning adequate incomes (McGoldrick, 1989; Rae, Jacobsen, & Blatter, 1991). Women, therefore, may have a harder time than men when they try to reorganize their lives (Rae, Jacobsen, & Blatter, 1991; Uhlenberg, Cooney, & Boyd, 1990).

Divorce may be repeated in successive generations. Women who were raised in families of divorce may choose to marry early and experience difficulty selecting appropriate mates. They were socialized with expectations for themselves and their place in the world which are no longer held by many others in society (Brown-Wilson & DeShane, 1983).

In early adulthood, divorce is typically a transitional state, followed by remarriage. "That is not the case after age 40, especially among women" (Hagestad, 1987, p. 187). Otten cites statistics from Uhlenberg and associates:

. . . remarriage declines sharply with age, with the rate falling to less than 3% after age 45. Moreover, record divorce levels among younger women in recent decades mean more women reaching mid-life are already divorced. (Otten, 1989, p. B1)

Recognizing the impact of divorce on older women, and the crisis of transition from married to single status, peer support groups provide restabilization.

"EXPANDING HORIZONS"

Consistently, more women than men have participated in the Expanding Horizons support group program. These women have attended weekly group sessions for six weeks and many have continued in the alumni groups. Their ages range from early 40s to late 60s. They are very cognizant of their ages and stages of life and do not want younger people in their group. They appreciate finding peers who are facing similar situations. For example, they often have to deal with problems concerning their adult children and grandchildren, attending holidays and other family events (with or without adult children and with or without aging parents), and coping with similarly aged ex-spouses and, in some cases, with their ex-spouses' new wives.

SCREENING

A telephone interview conducted by one of the group facilitators (psychotherapists) is required for participation in "Expanding Horizons." When someone appears very disturbed (e.g., is exhibiting psychotic symptoms), she or he is referred to a more appropriate resource.

DESCRIPTION OF PARTICIPANTS

The Expanding Horizons support groups consists of 90 women, 86 are white and 4 are black women, residing in Central Indiana, mostly middle class, who are separated or have recently obtained divorces after long term marriages of at least two decades or more. A few women are in second marriages, the first of which had also ended in divorce. The length of second marriages was considerably shorter than first marriages.

At the time of their participation in the support groups, some women had full or part-time employment which included various clerical, secretarial, and sales positions. Some were health care service providers including a medical assistant, a speech therapist, and several nurses. Some were trained as teachers, but had not returned to the profession since raising children, and one woman was practice teaching and completing her bachelor's degree. Several women became first time college students and many others were taking courses to enrich their lives or to develop new career options. A few women maintained their own businesses which included public relations, free lance writing, and jewelry sales. Of the remaining women attending these support groups, several were full-time homemakers or retirees. The retirees' positions ranged from factory work to clerical and professional employment.

Most of the participants had not initiated their respective separations and divorces. One participant, for example, stated that her husband wanted the divorce and the reason given was that he "just wanted not to be married." In a few instances, spouses said that they wanted a divorce, and several moved out, but then took no further action. After long periods of time without any action, the other spouses (the non-initiators) felt forced to begin divorce proceedings, even though they did not want the divorce. One woman stated that her husband wanted the divorce, but she initiated the proceedings because he had not contributed to the household for almost a decade after a prior reconciliation. Some made decisions to divorce with the realization that nothing would ever change, that things would not get better, and they would no longer live in unhealthy and unloving marital relationships. One participant, for example, separated after tolerating many years of physical and emotional abuse. Another cited alcohol and related problems for her decision to leave her spouse. A majority were displaced by younger women in the affection of their spouses. One member, whose husband had left for several years, eventually reunited with him. In almost every case, the group participant was the one who did not want the separation and divorce. What we do not know is the fate of the initiating spouse and the use of any divorce adjustment and peer support group services.

WEEKLY SESSIONS

Each of the six sessions is arranged around a specific topical outline. In addition, semi-structured problems or topics of interest may be addressed as group members feel the need. Sessions may also bring forth areas of vulnerability, both social and psychological, which are unique to separated or divorced people over 50.

Session I: Getting Acquainted

The focus is on helping members feel comfortable. Time is spent getting to know one another. Everyone completes personal information sheets which ask for name, address, number of years married, and name and address of counselor. Members agree to maintain the confidentiality of what is said within the group and the names of the participants. Members sign their names to the confidentiality agreement at the bottom of the information sheet.

Participants share their own situations and discuss their expectations of what they will obtain from the group. Homework consists of listing several goals to be accomplished in the next six weeks and specific ways of reaching those goals. Long term goals may also be included.

Session II: Goal Setting and Grief Stage Identification

Participants share their homework lists: specific goals and ways to reach them. Kubler-Ross's model is presented (Kubler-Ross, 1969), and members identify one or more stages which best describe where they are: denial; anger; bargaining; depression; acceptance. For homework, participants are asked to work on their goals and keep a diary of their progress.

Session III: Self-Esteem Building

After facilitators discuss the meaning of self-esteem, feedback from the group is encouraged. Participants are taught to identify and change "crooked thinking" and erroneous beliefs. Group members up-date their goals and discuss individual issues. Participants draw and later discuss pictures of the "self" in their individual self-esteem drawings. Homework is assigned for two reasons. These include developing and reinforcing self-help skills and motivating participants to move beyond themselves and their individual worlds. For homework, members are asked to (1) bring in a short story, poem, or something they have written about self-esteem to share with the group; (2) practice saying positive statements about themselves and (3) be ready to report back on their progress.

Session IV: Coping with Stress

After facilitators lead a discussion about stress, they help individuals focus on ways to manage stress and anxiety. Participants then identify their own reactions to stress. Homework consists of finding a different way of responding to a stressful situation and being prepared to report the new coping styles to the group.

Session V: Small Group Sharing Options

During this session, family of origin is examined and family genograms are drawn; relationships with adult children and extended family members are discussed; experts are invited to speak on specific topics, e.g., attorneys, insurance agents, career planners, financial managers.

Session VI: Goal Setting Recheck

Members look at their beginning goals and are encouraged to take pride in the progress they have made. Monthly alumni support group meetings and future plans for participants are discussed.

MONTHLY ALUMNI GROUP

Each month the "alumni" group selects a topic for discussion and application. Topics may include communication skills, attitude awareness, cognitive management, personality development, family group dynamics, beliefs, stresses of anticipation, personal development, interpersonal skills, and relationships with adult children.

EFFECTIVENESS OF THE SESSIONS

Though no quantitative studies on each session or on the whole group experience have been undertaken, the facilitators, through clinical insight, have observed significant changes in group members. Feedback from group participants and self-evaluations suggest the same. Participants come to the group with extremely low self-esteem. They believe themselves to be failures and express a tremendous amount of self-blame. The following words are shared by group members to describe their respective experiences: "emotional roller coaster ride"; "everything is over"; "emotional withdrawal"; "after tears, numbness"; "pit city"; "humiliation"; "guilty"; "worthless"; "shame"; "stuck"; "betrayal"; cheating"; "like a kick in the stomach"; "survival"; "frustration"; "rejection"; "bitterness"; "loneliness"; "loss," and "sadness." One member described her "anger," "grief," and "resentment": "Anger because I feel betrayed by an individual whom I had completely trusted. Grief over the loss of a relationship which was a central point in the majority of my life. And I resent not being able to do the things with my life now that I had planned . . . Working until 65 was never part of my plans or goals."

Throughout the six sessions it appears that these women experience increases in self-esteem and begin to describe themselves in more positive terms. "Basically I feel I am both physically and emotionally strong, intelligent, unique and interesting, trustworthy, hard-working, appreciative and sensitive," stated one member. Another said, "But–this is not a helpless person, or a lost person, or a stupid person. She knows that there is more than rain in the world–that out there somewhere, out from under that dark cloud, there is sunshine and flowers waiting for her."

Changes toward more positive self-esteem may also be attributed to the fact that affirmation of self and other is a shared value within the group. Additionally, esteem is raised as friendships develop between and among these women. The positive, affirming, and supportive attitude of the facilitators also contributes to the positive climate for growth and change.

These women also report that they do not feel as isolated after starting the group. They see their growth, understand their life situations better, blame themselves and others less, resolve problems, obtain a clearer direction, and make peace with their new roles as single women. They say they have learned new ways to apply rational thinking skills. As one group member shared, "If I start thinking negatively, I *force* myself to change my thoughts." They are more focused on what they can do with the remainder of their lives. "I'm really over the hurt and I've made a good full life–I have a job I like, I go out a lot, I have lots of friends and I'm basically happy," said one participant. They set limits better, experience less despair as the weeks go by, take charge of their lives, and report feeling more alive. Facilitators evaluate these changes by noting changes in body language, facial expressions, behavior, personality characteristics, and affect in womens' voices. In an early session, for example, a woman may cry throughout much of the time. Later on, by contrast, this same woman may still be tearful and express feelings of deep sadness, but she is not as overwhelmed by these feelings and is able to deal more effectively and competently with the issues and concerns facing her.

DISCUSSION

We view divorce as a crisis or transition in the life cycle. For older women, this crisis complicates their ability to cope with life cycle tasks of aging. As with most aging persons, they are anxious about growing older and with the advent of divorce, now worry about managing independently, feeling worthwhile, accepting themselves as single persons, and developing a sense of wholeness and usefulness. Symptoms of stress, anxiety, and depression are not uncommon among women who are struggling with this transition. Even some women who initiate their respective divorces feel depressed and wish that they had other options. Some researchers suggest that two years after divorce there is similarity in emotional adjustment between both the divorce initiator and non-initiator. Without additional stressors, younger men and women can usually make the necessary adaptation to new lifestyles within two to three years (Heatherington & Tryon, 1989). It has been suggested that the recovery period for older persons is typically five to seven years.

Adaptation to parental divorce is also faced by young adults. We have noted an absence of research regarding the impact of divorce on adult children. Wallerstein and Corbin (1989) noted that age and developmental stage were linked to childrens' responses to divorce. A study by both Cooney, Smyer, Hagestad, and Klock (1986) identified the following problems of college age young adults whose parents had recently divorced: loyalty conflicts, anger, and concerns about the future for their parents. Studies by both Cooney et al., (1986) and Booth and Edwards (1989) suggest that women have more emotional problems with regard to the divorce of their parents than do their male counterparts.

Developmental issues of young adulthood, which include the tasks of separating from family of origin and making one's own life, are complicated by the divorce of parents. Cooney et al., (1986) noted the vulnerability of young women who are closely linked with their mothers to empathize and become involved with the parental divorce. Also, recently divorced mothers of young women are in need of help in the transition to single life after long term marriages. Both mothers and daughters, in our opinion, can benefit from participation in peer support groups. A treatment goal is the enhancement of family stability by raising the esteem of mothers and daughters and improving and nurturing their relationships so that they can help one another. With increasing divorce in later life, there is serious concern about the economic and socio-emotional well-being of women now and in future generations. It may be that through these interventions, second and even third generations of older and younger women may be helped to improve the quality of their marital and family relations.

REFERENCES

Ahrons , C.R., & Rodgers, R.H. (1987). *Divorced families: a multi-disciplinary developmental view.* New York: W.W. Norton.

Booth A., & Edwards, J.N. (1989). Transmission of marital and family quality over the generations: The effect of parental divorce and unhappiness. *Journal of Divorce, 13,* 41-57.

Brown-Wilson, K.B., & De Shane, M.R. (1983, April). *Factors influencing adjustment to late-life divorce.* Western Gerontological Society Annual Meeting, Albuquerque, NM.

Cain, B. (1988). Divorce among elderly women: A growing social phenomenon. *Social Casework: The Journal of Contemporary Social Work, 69,* 563-568.

Carter, B. & McGoldrick, M.(1989). *The changing family life cycle A framework for family therapy.* Boston: Allyn and Bacon.

Chiriboga, D.A., Roberts, J., & Stein, J.A. (1978). Psychological well-being during marital separation. *Journal of Divorce, 2,* 21-36.

Cooney, T.M., Smyer, M.A., Hagestad, G.O., & Klock, R. (1986). Parental divorce in young adulthood: Some preliminary findings. *American Journal of Orthopsychiatry, 56,* 470-477.

Deckert, P., & Langelier, R. (1978). The late-divorce phenomenon: The causes and impact of ending 20-year-old or longer marriages. *Journal of Divorce, 1*(1), 381-391.

DeShane, M.R., & Brown-Wilson, K.B. (1981). Divorce in late life: A call for research. *Journal of Divorce, 4,* 81-91.

Gander, A.M. (1991). After the divorce: Familial factors that predict well-being for older and younger persons. *Journal of Divorce & Remarriage, 1*(2), 175-192.

Hagestad, G.O. (1987). Divorce. In G.L. Madden (Ed.), *Encyclopedia of Aging* (pp. 187). New York: Springer.

Hagestad, G.O., & Smyer, M.A. (1982). Dissolving long-term relationships: Patterns of divorcing in middle age. In S. Duck (Ed.), *Personal Relationships. 4: Dissolving Personal Relationships.* (pp. 155-188). New York: Academic Press.

Heatherington, E.M., & Tryon, A. (1989). His and her divorces. *The Family Therapy Networker,* November/December, 58-61.

Kitson, G.C. (1988). *The impact of age on adjustment for women at thirteen months post death or divorce.* Unpublished paper delivered at 41st Annual Scientific Meeting of the Gerontological Society of America, San Francisco.

Kubler-Ross, E. (1969). *On death and dying.* New York: MacMillan.

Longfellow, J. (1991, May). *Women and divorce at midlife vs. younger age: The study of depression, self-esteem and sex roles.* Paper presented for the American Association of Applied and Preventive Psychology, Washington, DC.

McGoldrick, M. (1989). Women through the family life cycle. In M. McGoldrick, C.M. Anderson, & F. Walsh (Eds.), *Women in families: A framework for family therapy.* (pp. 200-226). New York: W.W. Norton.

Miller, J.B. (1976). *Toward a new psychology of women.* Boston: Beacon.

Otten, A.L. (1989, January 24). People patter: More older women likely to be single. *The Wall Street Journal,* p. B1.

Rae, J., Jacobsen, J.J., & Blatter, C.J. (1991). Support groups for persons experiencing divorce in later life. *Behavioral Sciences & the Law, 9*(4), 477-486.

Schaie, K.W., & Geiwitz, J. (1982). *Adult development and aging.* Boston: Little, Brown.

Silverstein, O. (1988). Single women: Later years. In M. Walters, B. Carter, P. Papp, & O. Silverstein (Eds.), *The invisible web: Gender patterns in family relationships* (pp. 390-406). New York: Guilford Press.

Stern Peck, J. & Manocherian, J.R. (1989). Divorce in the changing family life cycle. In B. Carter & M. McGoldrick (Eds.), *The changing family life cycle: A framework for family therapy* (pp. 335-369). Boston: Allyn and Bacon.

Uhlenberg, P., Cooney, T., & Boyd, R. (1990). Divorce for women after midlife. *Journal of Gerontology: Social Sciences, 45,* S3-S-11.

Uhlenberg, P., & Myers, M.P. (1981). Divorce and the elderly. *The Gerontologist, 21,* 276-282.

United States Bureau of the Census (1990). *Statistical abstract of the United States.* Washington, DC: United States Government Printing Office.

Wallerstein, J.S., & Corbin, S.B. (1989). Daughters of divorce: Report from a ten-year follow-up. *American Journal of Orthopsychiatry, 59,* 593-604.

Weitzman, L. (1985). *The Divorce Revolution: The unexpected social and economic consequences for women and children.* New York: Free Press.

Real versus Reel World:
Older Women and the Academy Awards

Elizabeth W. Markson
Carol A. Taylor

SUMMARY. Curiosity about whether the phenomenon of three actresses aged 60 or over winning the Academy award for Best Actress in the 1980s represented a new trend or was rather a random occurrence prompted this paper. Had changing demographics and the new psychology of women impacted the near invisibility of "older" women in American film and the stereotypical roles of nag, hag, or poor old thing and family martyr? The sample is comprised of 1,169 actresses and actors nominated in four acting categories (Best Actress/Actor, Best Supporting Actress/Actor) for Oscars from 1927-28 through 1990. Ages of Academy Award nominees were chosen for study because they offer a finite sampling of performances from "prestigious" films over the last 63 years and provide an accessible data base. Among the significant results are: women over the age of 39 have accounted for only 27% of all winners for Best Actress since 1927, whereas men in the same age category accounted for 67% of the Best Actor awards. On the silver screen, a woman is "older" by the time she is 35. Her career ends as his career begins. To what extent does this reflect the real world and provide positive images for women as they age?

Throughout the twentieth century, film and culture have exerted a powerful influence on how women of all ages are perceived and how they perceive themselves. During the past two decades, a dearth of roles for women in American film has been noted. Nearly

---

Elizabeth W. Markson, PhD, is associate director of the Gerontology Center and research associate professor in the Department of Sociology at Boston University. She is also a family therapist in private practice in the Boston area. Carol A. Taylor, MA, is a psychotherapist, film buff, and AAMFT approved supervisor in the greater Boston area.

157

20 years ago, Haskell (1974) noted that portrayals of women in film had already diminished in the prior dozen years. In American film, older actresses have traditionally been even less visible than younger women and, when present, have had limited roles, most often portraying stereotypical viragos, "poor old things" or minor characters. Aversion to older women is not unique to the film industry; consider, for example, the numerous unflattering words for old women (eg., hag, crone, old bag) and the numerous mother-in-law jokes and comic strip depictions of menacing, ugly, or absurd old women. Far fewer old men are similarly characterized. The distaste in the United States for older women at least in part is a remnant both of European history when suspicion of witchcraft "fell on every old woman with a wrinkled face" (Fraser, 1984) and Puritan Massachusetts where those most likely to be condemned for witchcraft were poor older women, usually single or widowed, who had a reputation for annoying their neighbors (Demos, 1982).

At first glance, however, the films of the 1980s appeared to feature older women, heralding a change with three of the ten winners of the Academy Award for Best Actress age 60 or older. Was Hollywood responding to societal change? Specifically, was the "graying of America," with the rapid growth of the older population, increasing opportunities for older women in film? Was there a change from the usual practice of relegating older actresses to cameo or walk-on parts? And had the emerging new psychology of women impacted cinematic depictions mirroring gender stereotypes about older women in particular? These questions prompted further inquiry about the number of older actresses in film and the way in which they are represented. To examine the extent to which American films may reflect broader scale social changes, we undertook an analysis of Academy Award nominees and winners of the four categories best actor, best actress, best supporting actress, and best supporting actor from 1927 (the first year in which the Academy Awards were given) through 1990.

The decision to focus on Academy Award winners was guided by several considerations. First, since 1900, over 100,000 feature films have been produced–clearly an unmanageable number to analyze. Moreover, many of these, especially from the early days of film, have been lost or are not readily available. Second, focus on Academy Award nominees and winners provides a finite data source of a comparable number of actresses and actors in "prestigious" films encompassing a variety of genres: for example, *Disraeli* (biography), *Mildred Pierce* (drama), *My Fair Lady* (musical), *High Noon* (western), *Misery* (suspense/horror), and *The Goodbye Girl* (comedy). Third, although data on the ages of film stars is often inaccurate, we hypothesized that such information might be more readily available for those nominated for Academy awards.

Actors and actresses in 1,169 roles comprised the sample: 585 nominations for actresses and 584 actors nominated for Academy Awards 1927-1990. Three hundred ten nominations were for best actress, 309 for best actor, and 275 each for best supporting actress and actor. Although Academy Awards were introduced in 1927, it was not until 1936, the ninth year of the Oscars, that the category of best supporting actress/actor was added. Also in 1936, the number of nominees for each award was set at five for each of the four acting categories; prior to that time as the above totals indicate, the number of nominees for best actress/actor varied by gender and from year to year.

Data on ages of each actor and actress nominated were compiled from a variety of sources, including biographical and film directories, newspapers, and magazines. Although biographical data on film stars is riddled with inaccuracies, contradictions, and missing information, they provide the best currently available estimate of birth dates of Academy Award nominees available and a basis for which to analyze how older actresses (and actors) have fared in the past six decades of American feature films. Birth information could not be ascertained for two males and five females (less than 1%) of all nominees.

FINDINGS

In analysis, six questions were addressed: (1) Have there indeed been significant shifts in the proportion of older women and men nominated for Academy Awards over the past six decades? (2) To what extent do the ages of those nominated for Best Actress differ from those nominated for Best Actor and is there a significant age difference among winners by gender? (3) Similarly, to what extent do the ages of those nominated for Best Supporting Actress differ from those nominated for Best Supporting Actor and is there a significant age difference among winners by gender? (4) Are there significant differences in the proportions of older men and women winning in the Best versus the Supporting categories? (5) Has minority representation of both genders increased within the history of the Oscar? (6) And finally, to what extent does the reel world reflect the real world of American society?

Data were input into a pc and analyzed using the statistical package, *Stata 2.05*. In analysis, any significant differences in ages of actresses and actors were assessed using t tests and analysis of variance, and relevant significant findings are reported in parentheses.

Decade Trends. In April 1968 at the age of 60 when she won her second Oscar for Best Actress, Katharine Hepburn cabled the Academy's president, Gregory Peck, saying "They don't usually give these things to the old girls, you know" (Edwards, 1988, p. 355). She may not have known how accurate she was, for Hepburn and Marie Dressler, who won in 1930-31 at the age of 62, were the only two women 60 or over to win as Best Actress in the then 40 year Academy history. Hepburn later won two more Oscars as Best Actress, accounting for half the awards made to women over the age of 60. With the exception of Hepburn, older women nominees for Best Actress have been rare. Figure I summarizes the mean ages of actresses and actresses nominated for the Academy Award since its inception. As may be seen in the table, women with an average age of 37 over the 63 year period, have been consistently younger than men, whose average age was 43, a difference significant at the .0001 level. As may also be seen in the table, the difference between male and females has been remarkably consistent through the decades, with the exception of the 1980s when three actresses–Katharine Hepburn, Jessica Tandy, and Geraldine Page–inflated the total. Even given the Hepburn-Page-Tandy effect, an analysis of variance indicated no significant decade trend. If these three are omitted, the mean age of female nominees shows even more minor fluctuations over the decades.

Best Actress and Actor Nominees and Winners. In the 63 years of awards for Best Actress and Actor, the average (mean) age of nomi-

FIGURE I. AVERAGE AGE OF ACADEMY AWARD NOMINEES BY DECADE AND GENDER, 1927-90

DECADE	AVERAGE (MEAN) AGE	
	FEMALE	*MALE*
1920s	*31*	*41*
1930s	*37*	*39*
1940s	*36*	*44*
1950s	*35*	*40*
1960s	*39*	*41*
1970s	*36*	*45*
1980s	*39*	*47*
1990s	*41*	*44*
ALL DECADES	*37*	*43*

nees was 44 years among males with 67 percent between the ages of 35 and 53. Among females the average age was 35, with 67 percent between the ages of 23 and 47. Put differently, only 27 percent of female nominees for Best Actress were over the age of 39 compared to 67 percent of the men. (This trend continued in the 1991 nominations where the average age of best actress nominees was 35.6 and of best actors 48.8.)

Among those actually winning an Oscar, women over the age of 39 accounted for only 27% of all winners for best actress whereas men in the same age range account for 67% of the Best Actor winners (p = .0000). The average age for female Oscar winners during the 3 years of the 1920s was 29, for men 48–an almost 20 year difference. During the 1930s, the average age of winning actresses was 32 and of winning actors 40. Similar patterns persisted through the 1940s and 1950s for both genders. It was not until the 1980s that the average age of actresses winning the award increased to almost age 45–due not to an increasing appreciation of the gray-ing of America, but to the "Hepburn/Page/Tandy effect" in three films (*On Golden Pond, Trip to Bountiful,* and *Driving Miss Daisy*). If these three actresses are omitted from awards during the 1980s, the average age of female winners during that decade is very similar to the average for all decades. Indeed, in the first three years of the 1930s, three women (Marie Dressler twice, May Robson once) were nominated for best actress, the difference being that the three older women nominated in the 1980s won. Figure II summarizes the age groups of all performers winning the Academy award as best actress/actor since 1927.

In the 1980s, similar to preceding decades, half the female win-ners were under the age of 38 compared to half the men who were aged 45 or older, emphasizing that, even given the Hepburn/Page/Tandy effect, youth remained a powerful criterion for winning an

FIGURE II. AGE GROUPS OF ACADEMY AWARD WINNERS
FOR BEST ACTOR AND ACTRESS, 1927-1990

AGE OF BEST AT AWARD	PERCENT OF ACTORS (n=63)	PERCENT OF ACTRESSES (n=63)
UNDER 24	0	8%
25-29	0%	27%
30-34	9%	29%
35-39	24%	10%
40-44	32%	13%
45-49	14%	5%
50-54	8%	0
55-59	5%	0%
60-64	6%	6%
65 or over	2%	3%

award for women while middle age was an equally powerful criterion for award winning men. Once past the age of 59, however, nominations and winners drop for both genders. During the 63 years surveyed, no women aged 60 or over were nominated for best actress during the 33 year period 1933-1966, and no men aged 60 or over were nominated for best actor during the 29 years of 1930-1959. Among those aged 60 or over in the history of the Awards, a total of 13 men have been nominated 17 times (5% of the total nominees for Best Actor) with five winners and nine women nominated 12 times (4% of total female Best Actress nominees) with six winners, three of whom were Katharine Hepburn.

The types of roles portrayed by male and female nominees for Best Actress/Actor aged 60 or over, however, varied sharply. Males nominated but not winning as best actor depicted roles including family doctor, lawyer, judge, newspaper magnate, successful mystery writer, t.v. newsman, Jewish Nazi hunter, con man, and jazz musician. In contrast, roles played by female nominated but not winning as best actress included a shopkeeper, nanny, and pianist; none of these roles focussed primarily on their professional identities. Male Oscar winners portrayed a statesman (Disraeli), U.S. Marshal, tv reporter, and pool hustler. Only two men, one of whom was a former professor, were retired. All three of the roles by award winning females during the 1980s were of housewives or retirees.

Best Supporting Actress/Actors Nominees and Winners. Among nominees for supporting actor and actress, a gender-linked age pattern also was found. As among nominees for Best Actor/Actress, men were significantly older than women (p = <.0001). The average age among male nominees in supporting roles was 45, with 57 percent between the ages of 30 and 60; among women nominees, the average age of women nominees was 39 with 67 percent between the ages of 25 and 53. While ages of male nominees closely paralleled that of men nominated for Best Actor (45 versus 44), female nominees for Best Supporting roles were somewhat older than women nominated for Best Actress (39 versus 35), a difference statistically significant at the .01 level.

Among Oscar winners for supporting roles, women were, on the average, seven years younger than men winners (p = <.01). There were age differences for both genders between the Oscar winners for Best Supporting roles and those nominated but not winning. Although both men and women who won were older than non winners, this difference was significant only among men with an average age of 48 versus 41 for men (p = .01). There was only a two year difference in the ages of female winners versus nominees for Best Supporting roles; the average winner age was 41 and average age of non-winners 38. These findings suggest that opportunities for actresses are greater in peripheral roles than in leading roles as they age. Actors, however, are more likely to have both opportunities to play a leading or supporting role well into midlife. When is a woman "older?" On the silver screen, she is "older" by the time she is 35.

Minorities. Even less visible than women in their 40s or older are members of minority groups of either sex. As may be seen in Figure III, although the proportion of minority nominees has sporadically increased over 63 years, ethnic and racial minority actors and actresses remain amazingly unrepresented among Oscar nominees. Of the total number of nominations for the four categories of Oscar, only 38 nominees (seven for best actor, four for best actress, 13 for supporting actress, and 14 for supporting actor) have been identifiably Native American, African-American, Asian, or Latino. No male or female minority members were nominated for an Academy Award until 1939 (Hattie McDaniel who won for her supporting "Mammy" role in *Gone With the Wind*). Not until 1949 was a second minority nominated, again for supporting actress. Only four men and four women actually won an Oscar; seven of the eight being for supporting roles. The age pattern of minority actresses and actors follows that described above, favoring older men and younger women.

Today people of color account for about one in six Americans, but their frequency among Academy Award nominees or winners makes their rare appearance, like that of older women, assume a false prominence. It is precisely because parts for minority actresses and actresses are so infrequent that their roles are remembered.

REEL WORLD VERSUS REAL WORLD

As Mander noted almost two decades ago, "If politics is the present tense of history, media is the present tense of politics"

FIGURE III. MINORITY REPRESENTATION BY DECADE AND GENDER, 1927-90

	1920s	1930s	1940s	1950s	1960s	1970s	1980s	1990
BEST ACTRESS NOMINEES	-	-	-	1	-	2	1	-
BEST ACTRESS WINNERS	-	-	-	-	-	-	-	-
BEST SUPPORTING ACTRESS NOMINEES	-	1	1	3	3	-	4	1
BEST SUPPORTING ACTRESS WINNERS	-	1	-	1	1	-	-	1
BEST ACTOR NOMINEES	-	-	-	1	1	2	3	-
BEST ACTOR WINNERS	-	-	-	-	1	-	-	-
BEST SUPPORTING ACTOR NOMINEES	-	-	-	1	2	1	8	2
BEST SUPPORTING ACTOR WINNERS	-	-	-	-	-	-	3	-

(Mander, 1974, 68). Just as those more powerful judge which oc-
currences will be considered significant enough to be recorded as
history, so do they decide the ways in which women are portrayed
in film. Few older women appear in film and, when portrayed, are
almost exclusively in circumscribed, traditional feminine roles
presenting women with few positive models for their own life-long
development.

The film industry is not alone, of course, in its lack of attention to
female development, for the social sciences and medicine have paid
little attention to women's maturation as distinct from that of men.
It was not until 1978, for example, that a major longitudinal study
on normal aging included women in its sample. Models of midlife
and old age have primarily been developed by men studying
middle-class males, ignoring women's development as well as racial, class, and ethnic differences. Moreover, traditional definitions
of both female psychopathology and "normal" behavior have
evolved from male models and often questionable assumptions; the
association of "involutional melancholia" with menopause is but
one example (cf. American Psychiatric Association, 1952; Kaufert,
1985).

What are the normal developmental changes associated with aging for women? Various theorists have postulated that a cornerstone
of female development throughout the life course is their bond to
others. Miller (1976) has pointed out that women's desire for affiliation is key to their sense of self. Gilligan (1982) echoes this in her
research findings indicating that women make moral decisions
based on their relationships and attachments to others. In American
society, as in many others, females are groomed as the carriers of
human communication.

A greater strain toward androgyny beginning in midlife among
both genders has been noted; that is, women become more assertive, men more nurturant (Gutmann, 1985). On a similar theme,
Bakan (1966) has suggested that two fundamental modalities characterize all people throughout life: agency and communion.
Agency, a "masculine" quality, is characterized by self-protective-
ness, self-assertiveness, and self-expression; communion, a "feminine" characteristic, by attachment to others. Extending this view,
Block (1984) proposed that women at higher stages of ego and

moral development have integrated both agency and communion into their personality, enabling them to deal with the issues and challenges of midlife and adulthood.

In the film world, however, men are much more "integrated" or androgynous throughout the life course. American cinema not only celebrates male agency but also their communion with one another. Although portrayals of female "communion" with men and children have been depicted in film since its early days, women's relationships with one another have received relatively little coverage. Unlike men, who have entire film genres (westerns, gangster, war, and "buddy" pictures) dedicated to their relationships, even in the "women's movie" the focus has been almost exclusively on their relationships to men whether or not males are physically represented on the screen. *Thelma and Louise* has often been described in the press as a "female buddy picture," underscoring the lack of a women's film genre comparable to the male "buddy picture." (This film is also notable in that one of the "buddies" is played by an older woman–45 year old Susan Sarandon.) In the real world, however, women's friendships with one another provide a buffer throughout the life course, enabling them to cope with gender inequality, responsibilities of home and family, often dual demands of home and job, and transitions and events of later life (Francis, 1990).

The 1991 movie, *Fried Green Tomatoes,* is doubly striking inasmuch as not only women's affiliations with one another are portrayed but a frankly old woman (Jessica Tandy at 82) brings about positive change in the life of a middle aged one (Kathy Bates). Yet it is primarily through the mechanism of life review by Tandy's film character rather than action in the here-and-now that such change occurs. One implication of this is that once a woman is frankly old, life review is the only significant occupation left for her. What message does this convey to women for their own futures in later life?

Screen portrayals of women in general, but most specifically older women, exhibiting qualities of agency are most often denigrated. The older woman who would be independent is portrayed as childish and in poor health as in *Trip to Bountiful,* or as willful and stubborn yet in need of male protection to save her from herself as in *Driving Miss Daisy*. Despite the growing proportion of American women 35 and over in the labor force, with a few notable exceptions, in the reel world of Academy Award actresses, women's occupational involvement tends to be either invisible or minimized. In the few films in which women's careers have been somewhat salient such as *Mildred Pierce* or *Autumn Sonata*, emphasis has been placed on the negative impact of work pursuits upon family relationships. Among actresses 60 and over, roles in which women have a career or are working are rare, despite the fact that 15% of real world women aged 60 and over are in the labor force (U. S. Department of Health and Human Services, 1991). Those factors contributing to female malaise in later life, such as poverty and lack of economic opportunity, as well as societal devaluation, are generally ignored as are the strengths of experience, agency, and communion with one another.

Whether or not they are nominated for an Academy Award, the opportunities for screen appearances are relatively few for older actresses. There is no dearth of women 60 years of age or older to play roles; in 1989, for example, they comprised 11% of all female members of the Screen Actors Guild compared to their men age peers who accounted for 9% of male members. Also in 1989, female Screen Actors Guild members 60 and over earned a yearly average of $7,446 in 1989–$4,339 less than the yearly average earnings of $11,785 by women members under the age of 60 (a difference statistically significant at <.0001). Actors age 60 and over also make significantly less than younger men but more than younger women; in 1989, male Screen Actors Guild members 60+ earned an average of $14,013 compared to $16,413 by younger men: a $2,400 difference (p = .0001) (Screen Actors Guild, 1991). Clearly both ageism and sexism are present in the real world of Hollywood as well as the reel world, with females 60 or over earning an average of $6,567 less than their male age peers. Indeed, in 1989, actresses peak earning power was between the ages of zero to nine while male actors' earnings in the same year were highest among those 40-59 (Screen Actors Guild, 1990).

The picture grows darker still for all women. According to a report by the Screen Actor's Guild, women of all ages comprised only 29.1% of all feature films in 1989. As Cohen observed:

". . . men in film have retreated to their own clubhouse for a while, treating women with passive exclusion or active denigration" (1991, 39). Unlike Streisand's Yentl, Belle, the feminist animation heroine in *Beauty and the Beast,* has achieved financial and critical success in Hollywood. Perhaps strong, intelligent, independent heroines in Hollywood films are only allowed in fairy tales. Otherwise, as in *Thelma and Louise,* they are either killed in the screenplay or at the box office if they are filmed at all.

Looking behind the camera, of the 313 nominations for Best Director in the 64 history of the Oscar (including 1991) not one American woman has been nominated, although some women have managed to break through the glass ceiling and successfully direct acclaimed and high grossing films. As for writers, a recent Writer's Guild report indicated that white men, predominantly under the age of 40, have written 80% of films shown in the last few years. As little as 10 years ago, again according to the Writer's Guild, the highest wages were paid to writers in their 50s, but by 1987, the highest pay went to writers in their 30s. A "Hollywood Graylist" of writers age 40 and over severely limits opportunities for employment (Lehr, 1992). Young writers are sought to cater to the anticipated film audience; prevailing "wisdom" holds that the primary film audience is composed of 15-25 year old males.

Yet this young male audience comprises only about 8% of the total U. S. population. Only 19% of households headed by this young age group have discretionary income, amounting to an average per capita, after taxes, discretionary income of $30,124 in 1986 dollars. In contrast, men and women 60 and older, over one quarter of whom have discretionary income, constitute 17% of the population with a discretionary per capita, after taxes, income of $44,262 among 60-64 year olds, $38,968 among 65-69 year olds, and $32,344 among those 70 years of age or older (1986 dollars). And, paradoxically, the baby boomers are reaching and firmly settling into middle age. If current fertility and immigration levels remain relatively constant, the only age groups to experience significant growth in the next century will be those past age 55. The most rapid increase is expected between the years 2005 and 2025 when the baby boomers reach 60. As Americans grow older and older with females predominating in older age groups, the decision makers and power brokers in Hollywood remain males, growing younger and younger.

As the demographic profile of the United States changes, therapists can increasingly expect that their practices will be comprised primarily of older women. Therapists treating older women (and, in the reel world, older begins at age 35) must evaluate the extent to which their own assumptions as well as those of their patients reflect cultural stereotypes that older women have little value, are asexual and unattractive, and often are men manques. Perhaps then it is not surprising that one recent report suggests that a "depletion syndrome," characterized by feelings of worthlessness, no interest in things, sense of hopelessness, thoughts of death, dying and suicide, and loss of appetite, differentiates symptoms of late-life depression from those observed among younger women (Newmann, Engel, and Jensen, 1990). Whether the symptomatology of female depression changes with age and whether its prevalence increases in later life or is a continuation or resurgence of earlier depression remain debated in the literature. What is clear, however, is that the politics of film reflect and reinforce the notion that an older woman generally has outlived her usefulness. With a few rare exceptions, older women today, as in the past, remain nearly invisible in American films. When portrayed, they are stereotyped: argumentative, incompetent, suspicious, and stubborn as in *Driving Miss Daisy*, powerless and ill as in *Trip to Bountiful,* or all-accepting and self-sacrificing as in *On Golden Pond*. With such models for female behavior and for our own aging it is scant wonder that survey after survey finds that women are more depressed than men (Kennedy, Kelman, Thomas, Wisniewski, Metz, & Bijur, 1989; Skodel & Spitzer, 1983; Stewart, Blashfield, Hale, Moore, May, & Marks, 1991), and that older women admit to far more depressive symptoms than their male age peers (Markson, Wilking, Kelly-Hayes, Belanger, & Carpenter, 1991)! Therapists working with midlife and older women face the challenge of deprogramming their clients from the cultural messages that increasingly devalue them as they age.

A final personal note: Working on this project has been as ambivalent an experience as going to the movies for the past decades within our recollection. As female movie goers, we keep hoping to see depictions of women's relationships with one another that have some ring of authenticity to our own experience and that of other women. We also hope to see our beloved female (and male) stars with whom we grew up as well as our age peers on the screen. As they age, the female (but not male) stars virtually vanish from the screen into a black hole. The older we and they become, the more time elapses between their performances. When an "older" female star does appear in a film, she is either relegated to relatively little screen time she portrays a character that neither we, nor we suspect, most women, would choose to emulate as a model for our own present or future lives. The "women's pictures" we see, with rare exceptions, do not seem to ring true.

REFERENCES

American Psychiatric Association (1952). *Diagnostic and Statistical Manual of the American Psychiatric Association* (first edition). Washington, D.C.: American Psychiatric Association.

Bakan, D. (1966). *The duality of human existence.* Boston: Beacon Press.

Block, J.H. (1984). *Sex role identity and ego development.* San Francisco, CA: Jossey-Bass.

Cohen, J. (1991, June). Neomacho. *American Film,* pp. 36-39.

Demos, J. (1982). *Entertaining Satan: Witchcraft and the culture of early New England.* New York: Oxford University Press.

Edwards, A. (1988). *A remarkable woman.* New York: William Morrow and Company.

Francis, D. (1990). Friends from the workplace. In B.B. Hess & E.W. Markson, (Eds.), *Growing old in America.* New Brunswick, N.J.: Transaction Books: 465-480.

Fraser, A. (1984). *The weaker vessel.* New York: Knopf.

Gilligan, C. (1982). *In a different voice.* Cambridge MA: Harvard University Press.

Gutmann, D. (1985). Beyond Nurture: Developmental perspectives on the vital older woman. In J. K. Brown & V. Kerns (Eds.), *In her prime: A new view of middle-aged women* (pp. 198-211). South Hadley, MA: Bergin and Garvey.

Haskell, M. (1974). *From reverence to rape: The treatment of women in the movies.* New York: Holt Rinehart and Winston.

Kaufert, P.A. (1985). Midlife in the midwest: Canadian women in Manitoba. In J. K. Brown & V. Kerns (Eds.), *In her prime: A new view of middle-aged women* (pp. 181-197). South Hadley MA: Bergin and Garvey.

Kennedy G.J., Kelman, H.R., Thomas, C., Wisniewski, W., Metz, H., & Bijur, P.E. (1989). Hierarchy of characteristics associated with depressive symptoms in an urban elderly sample. *American Journal of Psychiatry, 146*(2), 220-225.

Lehr, D. (1992, January 26). Screen writers talk about Hollywood's graylist. *Boston Globe,* pp. B-37, 39ff.

Mander, A.V. (1974). Her story of history. In A.V. Mander, & A.K. Rush, (Eds.), *Feminism as Therapy* (pp. 63-88). New York: Random House.

Markson, E.W., Wilking, S.V., Kelly-Hayes, M., Belanger, A., & Carpenter, B. (1991, November). *Depression among the Framingham Cohort.* Paper presented at the 1991 Annual Meeting of the Gerontological Society of America, San Francisco, CA.

Miller, J.B. (1976). *Toward a new psychology of women.* Boston: Beacon Press.

Newmann, J.P., Engel, R.J., & Jensen, J. (1990). Depressive symptom patterns among older women. *Psychology and Aging, 5*(1), 101-118.

Screen Actors Guild. (1991). [Unpublished data]. Hollywood, California: Screen Actors Guild. (1990). *The female in focus: In whose image.* Hollywood, California: Screen Actors Guild (photocopy).

Skodol, A.E., & Spitzer, R.L. (1983). Depression in the elderly: Clinical criteria. In L. D. Breslau & M.R. Haug (Eds.), *Depression and aging: Causes, care, and consequences* (pp. 20-29). New York: Springer Publishing Company.

Stewart, R.B., Blashfield, R., Hale, W.E., Moore, M.T., May, F.E., & Marks, R.G. (1991). Correlates of Beck Depression Inventory scores in an ambulatory elderly population: symptoms, diseases, laboratory values, and medications. *The Journal of Family Practice, 32*(5), 497-502.

United States Department of Health and Human Services, Administration on Aging (1991). *What you should know about the aging of America* [photocopy] (March). Washington, D.C.: Administration on Aging.

Between Midlife and Old Age:
Never Too Old to Learn

Rachel Josefowitz Siegel

SUMMARY. This article is based on taped interviews with 56 women, individually and in groups, between the ages of 60 and 70, as well as my own experience as a woman past 65. Discussions with friends and colleagues in this age group also contributed to my thinking. My sense is that the seventh decade is one of numerous transitions in the lives of women, and that these transitions require extensive, varied, and often painful opportunities for learning. Furthermore, the proximity to life's ending also acts as a strong motivator for engaging in activities that had previously been put off; these include a variety of self-selected and often pleasurable learning experiences. The learning that takes place at this age is rarely acknowledged; it is more likely to be overshadowed by the ageist assumption that old people lose their ability to learn or even to comprehend new information, and by the sexist assumption that women are incapable of making intelligent and practical decisions. These interviews and informal discussions contradict such stereotypical misinformation about old women, showing instead a high level of personal and interpersonal learning, as well as the development of extensive and creative new coping strategies.

I expect growth until I die.

–Virginia Rinker

Rachel Josefowitz Siegel, MSW, is a 67 year old recently widowed feminist therapist, lecturer, and writer living in Ithaca, NY. Her primary interests are old women and Jewish women. She hereby credits and appreciates all the women, named and unnamed, who spoke so openly about their feelings and life experiences.

SEEKING LIFE'S MEANING
IN A WORLD THAT MAKES US INVISIBLE

The decade of the 60's represents a transitional stage of life between midlife and old age, which requires a fundamental change in how we see ourselves and how we experience our place in the world. Our inner growth is profound. We are deeply engrossed in reassessing our life goals, our values, our priorities. In the words of Shevy Healey, white Jewish lesbian and retired therapist: "I feel like I'm on this quest and there's a deadline; the quest has to do with finding out what it's all about." We are engaged in making significant choices affecting the quality of our lives while we are also making choices about the end of life. We are putting our house in order, both spiritually and practically, so that we can live more fully now before we die.

Taped interviews were conducted with 56 women in their 60's; 20 women individually, and 36 women who met in 4 distinct focus groups (see appendix). Several friends and colleagues in this age group also shared their thoughts and feelings on this topic. Each group and each woman talked with some intensity about an inner shift or an inner struggle. One group related this inner process to spirituality, seeing it as an everpresent process of awakening to what and who we truly are.

Dora Fratelli, white, married retired teacher, counselor and former theological student was especially interested in this topic: "This is the time of life when a woman can develop in that area (spirituality) without so much concern about what's happening in the workplace." Finding a life meaning, identifying who we are at the beginning of old age, emerged as one of the key issues among participants in this project.

Our search for meaning takes place in a world that treats us as if we were not there: " . . . invisible . . . in that people walk into me, it's amazing! . . . I'm a big woman, you can't miss me! But people do seem to walk right past me." Polly Taylor, self-employed white lesbian mirrored the words of many other women. Emalu Lee said : "We're never in the picture," and the women in her group of displaced homemakers nodded in agreement. Perhaps that is why so many of the women I interviewed gave me permission to use their names. It was a way to become visible, to be heard.

Personal growth and the relational changes of this life stage occur within the context of deep losses and shifts in existing relationships, a body that can no longer perform at the familiar level that we have come to expect, and a social atmosphere that is disrespectful of old age in women and makes us appear invisible, stagnant, ludicrous, or burdensome.

FACTS AND FEARS ABOUT SENILITY

Gerontologists and social scientists are beginning to challenge the stereotypical assumptions about old people's inability to learn. Such findings tend not to have much impact on the prevailing ageist beliefs and attitudes that surround us. The false notion that old folks lose their ability to learn, to absorb new facts, or to form new relationships, is entrenched in our culture as well as in our own minds. Interviewees reported many incidents of age-related patronizing, and discounting, especially among legal, medical, and mental health professionals.

Our fears, both realistic and exaggerated, about losses of memory, approaching senility, and Alzheimer's disease, may get intensified by ageist assumptions, and can cause us to approach new tasks with excessive doubts and undue hesitation. Most interviewees were concerned about forgetting more names and numbers than they used to and having to write things down a lot. Women said things like: "You wonder how fast your mind is going to go (anon)," and someone else: "I have difficulty changing my train of thought . . . can't seem to focus on so many things . . Things like that scare me more than physical ailments (anon)," also: "I lose my train of thought . . ."

The realistic potential for impending limitations, and the tendency to exaggerate or generalize our natural memory losses can have some paralyzing effects on individual women; on the other hand, such awareness can also become a motivator for doing now what we've always meant to do some day. Some women were aware that age-related short-term memory limitations do not interfere with our ability to learn new facts or behaviors. Others were more likely to lump all misinformation about late life learning under a generalized fear of approaching senility.

INNER GROWTH DURING TRANSITIONS

For many women, the post-retirement years offer an opportunity to explore and develop previously dormant aspects of creativity; for others, it is a time of painful adaptations. Many women find that they experience extremes of involvement with people or projects, alternating with periods of isolation.

The themes of learning and personal growth were consistently at the forefront of my interviews. Major changes and transitions in our personal circumstances present us with the need to learn new ways of coping. We also have new opportunities and often feel increased motivation or desire to explore areas of learning that may have been set aside during earlier years.

When our bodies give us undeniable evidence of approaching old age, and society no longer treats us like young or middle-aged women, our need to respond creatively to our own aging triggers new growth and learning on many levels. We learn to live with diminishing physical capacities and with the tensions and uncertainties that are inherent in living closer to the end of our lives.

Retirement provides the time and leisure to make new choices, and the proximity of death or infirmity creates an urgency to do things now instead of putting things off. Many women become widows in their 60's, since male partners were typically five to ten years older in our generation, and the average life expectancy for men is 74. The painful and complex transition to widowhood means learning a whole new way of life, in many cases living alone for the first time in adult life. Women who had recently lost a partner reported feeling a deep inner isolation or loneliness, even while engaged in meaningful activities.

In group and individual interviews we often talked about how to value ourselves, our bodies, our minds, our activities, when our society does not give us any indication of valuing us. Self-doubts arose especially in times of crisis and during personal losses. Discussions centered around such questions as: "how do you make your time valuable? what are you worth without goals? is it ok to do less rather than more?" We did not always agree, but we were all deeply engaged in the process of making new sense of our lives. "I've been busy *doing, doing* all my life, and thinking back at the kind of inner life that I've had, I've really been at odds with what I am. I've been *doing*, what I've wanted is *to be*. not *to do* all the time. So my goal is *to be* from here on out," said Virginia Rinker, a married white retiree engaged in community organizing. Another woman said: "I'm not ready to stop doing, I got such a late start doing what I wanted to do . . the kind of work that is meaningful to me. I feel right in the middle of it, yet I also want more time for myself, for reflection and quiet contemplation (anon)."

The sexagenarians who were still in the work force and had no noticeable time for reflection were also engaged on some level in this process of shifting life priorities and finding new meaning in life. "I want more time to smell the flowers," said my friend Theo Sonderegger, a professor of psychology, who was at that time responsible for the care of her dying husband and her elderly mother.

EXTERNALLY IMPOSED LEARNING: COPING WITH THE KNOWLEDGE OF APPROACHING DEATH

In our 60's, more than ever before, illness or disability are likely to affect us and the people we care about. We learn new ways of coping with difficult health conditions and we learn about giving care to a less able partner, relative, friend, or neighbor. Our more frequent exposure to physical and mental disabilities forces us to rethink our attitudes and our able-bodied biases.

We also learn to live with the profound uncertainty of not knowing how or how soon we will die and how much care we will need to provide or to receive. This uncertainty affects our moods, our personal interactions, our financial planning, and every aspect of our lives. "One of the things about being our age is that we don't know (anon)." Celia Bolyard, a married, white realtor, said: "We have done some planning . . . for instance a living will . . . put our assets in trust. . . . so having done these things, we are ready to live . . . I wish I knew; if I thought I had two years left to live would do a lot of different things . . . if I knew that I don't have to worry about my old age. I'd like to go on trips, buy a new car." Another woman spoke of her sense of not knowing as follows: "I wonder if I'm going to be a widow or if my husband is going to outlive me . . . that's kind of important to me."

In each of the groups we talked at length about our preparations for possible infirmities and our practical preparations for death. I sensed that our fear of death and of the process of dying was reduced somewhat as we became more knowledgeable and the topic became more familiar. Sadly, during the seven years of this project, we also learned a great deal about coping with the accumulated deaths of significant people in our lives, including three women who had participated in two of the groups. The project's participants differed significantly in personal attitudes and preferences. We did not agree about how to best cope with our losses and with the inner shift toward approaching the end of life. While some of us found comfort and relief in talking repeatedly about the recent deaths of loved ones, others preferred to be more private.

Women whose partners had died spoke of periods of feeling profoundly isolated and disconnected from friends who were still coupled; they found support primarily among other survivors. Lu Chaikin, a white lesbian therapist, spoke most poignantly of her inner growth while working with AIDS patients: ". . . when you're dealing with death so closely, everything gets turned upside down . . . What I've discovered . . . it pushes me much more into the present moment . . . it forces me to live much more."

When our style of mourning and of absorbing our losses differs from that of others, we feel a sense of otherness or separation from close friends or family. At such times, the learning to cope with differences can be painful indeed.

NEW CHALLENGES: MEDICAL, LEGAL, FINANCIAL

The field of health care has changed dramatically during recent years, and the skills that we had acquired in getting the right kind of medical attention are not necessarily useful anymore. The helping professionals who are our age and whom we had trusted over the years have now retired or died. We have to learn to relate to professionals who are younger, who have different styles of communicating, and who are likely to discount our own observations or make ageist assumptions about what is good for us. In this age of new technologies and conflicting medical opinions, it is not easy to get the kind of information we need from our health-care providers, especially if they assume that we are too old to understand.

The stresses of unfamiliar medical procedures and the complexities of filling out insurance forms confront us at times of crisis or illness when we are not functioning at our best. We need also to become familiar with the medicare and social security systems. Many of us must learn to do these chores for others as well as for ourselves and that includes finding out where we can get help and advice on these matters. Contrary to common belief, women of our age may have less to learn in this area than men. Marilyn Strassberg of the Ithaca Office for the Aging reported: "They (women in their 60's) may be managing health care and insurance payments and claims and all that sort of thing for someone in their 80's and that's a fairly common thing . . . There are a lot of women's jobs, clerical jobs, where they deal with money and papers, so I don't think we have as many women coming in who have never touched anything like that as we did maybe ten or twelve years ago . . . more women reaching age 60 or 70 now have had work experience as secretaries."

Single or married, rich or poor, when we approach retirement, we need to reassess our financial situation, perhaps make decisions about investments and about selling our home or converting it into income producing space. Economic realities probably make the most difference in what an individual woman's options are and how secure she feels about herself and the rest of her life. A woman's sense of financial security, however, does not depend entirely on her monetary assets. I asked each respondent if she was concerned about her financial security; the answers varied as much according to the particular woman's personal value system and personality as they did according to the financial value of her assets. A Native American interviewee who chose to remain anonymous replied: "I probably should be concerned, but I'm not . . . I don't have any wants. I don't owe any money. I'll get along." She viewed her retirement as an opportunity to return to the cooperative and nature loving, holistic values of her people. Other women felt that money was one of their primary concerns. The displaced homemakers in our sample, who could not afford to retire, and who had no assets to speak of, had to learn to juggle their social security and sometimes their disability checks along with their limited opportunities for partial employment just to survive.

Retirement and estate planning are stressful and require us to think and speak about our own and our partner's death, a skill that most of us have not previously practiced. New and intimidating fields of information are involved. Some of the women who had previously handled their own financial matters quite independently now needed to make decisions that challenged their well established sense of competence. New widows are faced with unexpected and often unpleasant legalities and an accumulation of time-consuming and unfamiliar forms and decisions at a time of emotional turmoil. In our generation, many lesbian relationships are still secret, and a lifetime partner is unprotected by law unless special arrangements have been made; this process raises difficult dilemmas for lesbian couples.

Women with a partner or a spouse deal with the emotional and practical tasks of talking with each other about what plans to make regarding death. Making joint decisions may bring out the weaknesses in communication and the power inequities that exist within the relationship. On the other hand, the strengths of the relationship may also surface and the couple may gain a sense of security and closeness by handling these matters together.

The learning that takes place when we cope with unfamiliar legal, financial, and medical matters is usually not recognized or acknowledged. We tend to be more aware of how poorly we seem to handle these things, rather that how impressive it is that we are handling them as well as we are.

NEW OPPORTUNITIES

Retirement brings on new opportunities for learning. Structuring our days in retirement is a process that is not as simple as we expected it to be. Marian Reeves, a recently retired white teacher, living alone, felt shy about confiding: "When I was getting ready to retire I was all excited about the things I was going to be able to do. Well it didn't work out that way. I seemed to be in a state of loss, I couldn't get motivated to do these things I had planned on doing."

Not everyone responds to retirement with the same sense of loss. Some women feel relief from the tensions of the workplace. Those who move to a new community after retirement have to learn new ways of adjusting to the physical and social climate of that new location.

Contrary to the assumption that this life stage is one of limited choices and fewer opportunities, many of us chose to do new things and to expose ourselves to new experiences. Financial and health circumstances make a difference in our range of opportunities for self-selected learning at any age. The large number of women living with illness and in poverty are much more limited in their choice of new experiences than the women who are in good health and financially comfortable. All the women interviewed were involved in new projects or working as volunteers, acquiring new information and applying old skills to new situations. Some were exploring new areas of creativity for which they had not found time before.

Carol Skinner is in her second marriage; she became a psychotherapist in her 40's. She expressed a new urgency in her 60's about doing things while we still can: "Now . . . I no longer wait till the chores are done . . . I feel the pressure of *'if I don't do it now.'* I am no longer going to *not* do these things I've been wanting to do." Her words were echoed by many others.

Emalu has published a book of her newly written poems; Betty and Laura took a study-tour to Antarctica; Charlotte and her husband attend a different Elder Hostel every year; Bev gave herself a cruise in Norwegian waters for her 60th birthday; Lael is taking piano lessons and has given two recitals. Carol learned Italian before spending a sabbatical year in Rome, where she also renewed her old love of painting and is now enrolled in a painting course.

Shevy Healey and Vera Martin took on leadership roles in creating the Old Lesbians Organizing Committee. Lydia Peyton tutors children in her granddaughter's elementary school. Lucille Parker, an African-American civil service retiree, helped create new projects at her senior center; she said:" Some of the programs need to be changed because we're past the age where 60-year olders are going to sit down and do nothing . . . you're going to want to keep moving or do something. You've got to find things to do and there's a lot out there to do. A lot to do." These women conveyed a vibrant sense of living fully and caring deeply about the world. Many women spoke knowingly about current politics and considered themselves committed activists, engaged in working for what they believed.

KEEPING UP WITH TECHNOLOGICAL CHANGES

We all have to learn new skills to keep up with the rapidly changing technology of our era; we did not grow up in an age of computers, VCRs, programmable phones, and microwave ovens, and we did grow up in an age when our gender role socialization taught us to mistrust our own ability to respond to mechanical objects. This means that we now have to think about whether we wish to live the rest of our lives without these conveniences or whether we wish to acquire the technical skills to operate the electronic gadgets of our time and overcome some deeply ingrained fears and hesitations about our own ability to do so.

MAKING OUR OWN CHOICES

By choice or of necessity, we learn a lot during this decade of transitions. We are confronted with many choices and have many opportunities to learn even more. We are also confronted with other people's expectations of what they would like us to learn. Times have changed, our social climate is very different from that of our youth. The familiar coping patterns and communication patterns of our earlier years are no longer in vogue. We are frequently exposed to new styles of speaking and of interacting. We sometimes feel pressure to conform to our childrens' or grandchildrens' ways of being in the world, and may or may not wish to do so. The interviews conveyed strong convictions and personal preferences in many areas. "I have become more inclined to speak out and to be less concerned about the reactions of others," (anonymous) was a statement that speaks for many. Some women were more eager to try new things in some areas but not in others, and some felt that they should be more adventuresome. Other women felt more certain about their right to decide not to try new things if they did not feel like it, and resented being expected to do so. Women were afraid of being perceived as a stereotypical old woman set in her ways. It is important to distinguish between what we chose to learn and what others want us to learn. As we get older, we continue to learn not to let others define who we are and what is important to us; we continue to learn to value our selves and our decisions on our own terms and not by other people's standards.

INTERPERSONAL GROWTH

Death and illness are powerful motivators for interpersonal learning, and we are not too old to make significant changes in how we interact with the people we love. The awareness of death brings us closer to not putting off what we want to do as a couple or to say what we've wanted to say to each other. Some couples learn at this stage of life to be more mellow with each other, more accepting of each other's limitations, or to express their feelings more openly without holding on to bad feelings as long as they used to. "We still fight, but there is more willingness to compromise. It seems less important to win the point and more important to feel close again (anon)."

Some of us become clearer about what is important in our lives and who we want to relate to more intimately. Many of us form new relationships, especially new friendships with women. Three of the four groups that participated in this project have continued to meet for friendship, support, and further discussion. We learn to be more selective in our social life. We feel an urgency to take care of unfinished emotional business while we are still capable, to say what we've been wanting to say to our partners, our children, our friends, or to do what we've been wanting to do with a particular person. We may run into some difficulties when the other person is not ready to make that shift with us. When that happens, we may have to learn to cope with some painful feelings of frustration and rejection.

Our relationships shift as we move through the losses and disconnections imposed by our age–the end of paid employment, the loss or diminishment of our own faculties, the separations due to travel and changes of locale, and the death of age-mates, old time friends, partners, and family members. With each illness or infirmity among our friends and associates, we learn something more about care-giving or about accepting and asking for help. Whether we speak of independence, self-sufficiency, or competency, our understanding of these concepts changes as we strive to retain self-esteem while needing the help of others and as we watch others go through that process. Our learning task, as we move into old age, is to continue to accept ourselves, even as our bodies start to malfunction, and even when we are in physical or emotional pain and feel like complaining. We live in a society that worships physical perfection and accomplishments and that despises 'weakness' of any kind. As our bodies weaken and are less perfect than they were, we tend to feel more disconnected from the way we think we should be and from what our environment admires. The learning may be very painful, but if we are lucky we do learn to shift our sense of self-acceptance away from the myth of perfect independence and closer to the reality of interdependence. We learn to accept ourselves as people who are not completely self-sufficient and who are no longer able to do for others to the same extent that we and they have come to expect of us.

With each death of a loved one and of an intimate or casual acquaintance, we learn something more about who we were within that relationship and who we are without the presence of that person. With each loss we also learn something more about death and about dying and about how to cope and survive.

Call it wisdom, or call it life experience; our late life learning adds to an inner sense of knowledge about ourselves and about our place in the universe.

APPENDIX

A total of 56 women participated in this study.

1. Twenty women in individual, taped interviews lasting about two hours each.
2. Seventeen women in two groups: (a) the first six months of my own support group of 12 women over 60, now in it's seventh year, (b) a therapy group of five women over 60, lasting nine months, still meeting occasionally.

3. Nineteen women in two taped focus groups: (a) a ten session workshop involving 15 women, entitled Between Midlife and Old Age, offered at the Ithaca Womens' Community Building, still meeting twice a month on their own, (b) an eight session workshop for five displaced homemakers, co-led by Emmalu Lee of the Tompkins County Displaced Homemakers' Committee.

The groups all met in Ithaca, N.Y. Individual interviews took place in Ithaca, N.Y., Rochester, N.Y., Long Island, N.Y., Seattle, WA, and the San Francisco Bay Area, CA. Interviewees included four African-American women, two Native Americans, one Japanese-American raised in the U.S., one Filipina American immigrant, and 48 women of varied white ethnic backgrounds. Of the six lesbian women, two were closeted. Fifty women lived heterosexual life-styles. The five displaced homemakers lived at or below poverty level, two women lived in great affluence, the majority lived within the broad range of middle class circumstances.

The Empowerment of Women Residents in the Nursing Home

Janet Lee
Marylea Benware Carr

SUMMARY. The issues and concerns of old women as a group tend to have been overlooked by clinicians and academics who otherwise are committed to improving the quality of women's mental health care. In particular, the rich knowledge, experiences, and needs of women in nursing homes has largely been ignored. Our central goal in this project is the empowerment of women residents in nursing homes through self-esteem work, reminiscence, peer networking, and staff training, as well as the articulation of needs and choices and the initiation of self-identified institutional changes. We emphasize the intimate connections between the control that women have over the material conditions of their everyday lives and their mental health generally. We encourage clinicians and academics to work

Janet Lee, PhD, is Director of Women Studies at Oregon State University in Corvallis, OR. She teaches a variety of courses in Women Studies, including Women and Aging, and is currently involved in a project collecting oral histories of old women's experiences of menarche or first period. Marylea Benware Carr is a student in the Women's Studies program at Mankato State University in Mankato, MN. A graduate of the University of Illinois with a BS in Communications, she is currently a graduate teaching assistant with classes in introductory women's studies, women and self esteem, and women and assertiveness.

This project was funded by a grant from the Minnesota Women's Fund and the Southeastern Minnesota Initiative Fund and coordinated through the Region 9 Area Agency on Aging Senior Leadership Project. The authors would like to thank Debra Heise and Melissa for their role in organizing the project and their guidance and good humour. The authors' thanks go to all the workshop participants who shared themselves with us and taught us so much about human dignity. Dr. Lee would also like to thank those trusty souls in the Women's Writing Group at Oregon State University for their perceptive comments on an earlier draft of this paper.

as advocates for old women in the nursing home in order to preserve
the dignity deserving of all.

INTRODUCTION

When I am an old woman I shall wear purple . . .
And run my stick along the public railings
And make up for the sobriety of my youth.
I shall go out in my slippers in the rain
And pick the flowers in other people's gardens
And learn to spit.

These lines from the poem "Warning" by Jenny Joseph (1987,
p. 1) were almost always met with a smile or a chuckle by women
residents in the nursing home. This poem on dignity and resistance
evoked much pleasure and admiration. It represents the spark and
spirit alive in many nursing home residents, a desire for self-expression, autonomy and control over their lives and bodies. In this essay
we will share our experiences of a project aimed at improving the
mental health of women residents in the nursing home. We will
describe aspects of the workshops, emphasizing how women's control of the material conditions of their lives are intimately connected
to their mental health. In exploring visions for change, we suggest
the need to become advocates for old women, articulating their
needs, celebrating their strengths and contributions, and working
for structural changes in both nursing homes and society generally.

The issues and concerns of old women as a group tend to have
been neglected by clinicians and academics who are otherwise committed to improving women's status (MacDonald & Rich, 1983;
Russell, 1987). In particular the rich knowledge, experiences and
needs of women in nursing homes has largely been ignored (Doress
& Siegal, 1988; Smyer, 1989). With these issues in mind, we
launched a pilot project aimed at improving the mental health of
resident women through a series of therapeutic and educational
workshops. In order to encourage community building and networking, the workshops (meeting for two consecutive mornings)
were organized at a central nursing home site and included women
residents from several different homes within the region. No staff

were present during these workshops in order to provide residents with as much freedom of expression as possible. The staff also met for a staff training after the completion of the residents' workshops. These units were repeated in five different locations, representing a nine county region of South Central Minnesota.

Attendance at the residents' workshops varied, with a low of eight at one location and a high of 45 at another. The nursing home staff, primarily Activity Directors, selected participants on the basis of residents' cognitive and emotional functioning and general levels of health. Participants varied in age from early 60s to over 100 years, with most women in their mid 80s. Racial and ethnic diversity was very low and reflected the homogeneity of the nursing home population in this part of Minnesota, a region settled mostly by Scandinavian and German people. Almost all participants were white women and over two-thirds were rural working to middle class. Staff attendance at the staff trainings ranged from 12 to almost 100 participants, and included nursing, administrative and housekeeping staff. About 90% of staff participants were female, with a few male administrators and orderlies in attendance.

We emphasize that this project was aimed at empowering resident women, yet this word "empowerment," popular in its current fashionable use, needs to be defined. While we do use it to refer to individual psychological self-growth, self-assertion, and improvement in self esteem, it also connotes more than this. We emphasize that empowerment begins when individuals are able to understand the context of their lives, their access to and experience of both privilege and exploitation, and the ways that they might act to change the conditions of their lives. This involves a sense of personal control and awareness of constraint and choice that can promote psychological health.

Studies have shown that when nursing home residents experience a sense of their personal power, self esteem and motivation are enhanced, mental clarity and activity levels increase, and depression and mortality rates decrease (McDermott, 1989, p. 155). This awareness of empowerment as involving both a growth in personal efficacy and an understanding of self in the context of systemic forces is a basic tenet of feminist therapy and feminist education; it is also the goal of feminist consciousness-raising generally in its desire to promote the understanding of personal and political realities and the connections between these in new ways (Greenspan, 1983; Sturdivant, 1980; Young-Eisendrath & Wiedemann, 1987). It was from this perspective that we ran the workshops. We hoped that the educational component would provide meaningful and useful knowledge that related to participants' everyday lives in such a way as to spark ideas and strategies for personal and social change.

SELF ESTEEM AND SELF AWARENESS

Since the nursing home environment tends to be custodial rather than therapeutic, it does not facilitate autonomy and self control (Taft and Nehrke, 1990). Nursing home routines and the loss of personal space and possessions can exacerbate a feeling of loss of personal control and can promote psychological and physiological deterioration (Weisberg, 1983). This is also complicated by the fact that nursing homes are serving an older and more disabled population (Wells & Singer, 1985). We felt that it is crucial for nursing home personnel to provide an environment that meets residents' psychosocial needs and allows them dignity and self-respect. This was a goal of the residents' workshop.

We began this workshop with introductions of ourselves and participants. The women were asked to share something special about themselves they would like others to know, something which made them unique. We then went on to talk about self esteem, its sources and manifestations and to facilitate a discussion on this topic. Important here, we felt, was the need to integrate a dialogue on the negative stereotypes about aging which all, young and old, are encouraged to internalize. How rarely we encourage (for fear of offending or because we lack ways to articulate this) such honest discussions of the effects of internalized ageism on the elderly. Similarly, we found it important to talk openly about the internalization of a socially constructed "femininity." Why are we so modest about our achievements? Why is it so difficult to recognize and claim our accomplishments? Being able to name these processes can be empowering; it can give words and structure to generalized emotions. We discussed the connotations associated with such words as "old woman," and how using "older" or "elderly" are euphemisms that illustrate ageism and sexism.

We found affirmations to be effective and useful as self-esteem builders since they are tangible and accessible statements, that, in changing our thoughts, can change our emotions. We had an "affirmation bag," a shiny reflecting bag that picked up the light and irridesced different colors of the rainbow. It was full of individual statements which, we explained, were like fortune cookies without the cookie. These said such things as "I am a valuable and important person, and I'm worthy of the respect of others," or "I have choices that I can make and I have the right to make them," or simply "I am fantastic." The women picked out an affirmation and read it aloud to the group. This was usually accompanied by clapping and cheers of encouragement and comments by the other women. Most women tended to keep and remember their affirmations and refer to them at other times during the workshop.

Lyman and Edwards (1989) in their work with American Indian elderly found that the use of poetry in nursing homes was most effective in stimulating creativity and giving residents permission to feel pain and sorrow as well as joy and pleasure. Similarly Koch in *I Never Told Anyone* (1977) discusses poetry's relationship to empowerment in the nursing home setting. We used a lot of poetry, and with positive results. For example in the poem "Warning" mentioned above, there is a repetition of "when I am an old woman I shall wear purple" as a metaphor for autonomy, self reliance, and self control. We were delighted to see several women proudly wearing purple on the second day of the workshops, visibly affected by the poem. We shared several poems from the *Women and Aging* anthology (Alexander, Berrow, Domitrovich, Donnelly, & McLean, 1986), which depicted positive and creative images of old women, emphasizing their strengths and power.

An important component of the workshop was our use of reminiscence or life review strategies to articulate and celebrate the uniqueness and strength of individual women. Much research has been done on the effects of reminiscence on increasing cognitive and affective abilities, reducing depression and improving self esteem (Cook, 1984; Butler, 1963; Merriam, 1989; Rattenbury & Stones, 1989; Romaniuk, 1983). Providing the context where women can review their life experiences, choices and lack of choices, their strengths and achievements can be crucial in overcoming the learned passivity and helplessness of the nursing home environment (Brody, 1990). The specific reminiscence themes we chose involved leadership roles in community work, church or family; memories of important strong women in their lives who are remembered with special fondness as role models, mentors or guides; and recognizing, accepting, and celebrating diversity. We chose these themes in order to help participants articulate, value, and celebrate strengths, achievements, and skills which they or other women had and have. We used guided imagery techniques to help the women ground themselves and feel relaxed enough to start remembering. A crucial point here is made by Perschbacher (1984, p. 343) who emphasizes "In order for activity programs to have therapeutic relevance, they must take the residents' strengths and life tasks as a focal point."

We also used some audio-visuals–one entitled "Ruth Stout's Garden" was especially well-received. It tells the story of Ruth Stout, an independent, free-thinking woman in her 80s. Her garden and the way she plants and harvests are metaphors for the way she leads her life as a caring, autonomous, and self-reliant old woman. Another film, "One Fine Day," a short (six minutes), up-beat representation of women in history, was effective for our reminiscence theme on diversity. It is fast moving with pleasant music and gives a strong visual effect of the remarkable contributions of different kinds of women. Initially we were concerned that the use of poetry and audio-visuals that symbolize bold declarations of independence might highlight the lack of autonomy available to the women in the nursing homes, and, in accentuating the restrictive nature of their situation, possibly lead to feelings of helplessness and despair. What we found tended to be the opposite; the residents talked about these autonomous women with admiration and respect and tended to see them as role models.

The effects of these two mornings on the women involved in the workshop was for the most part positive in that they verbalized their enthusiasm and pleasure to us and to the staff, and appeared alert, interested, and moved by the self-work in which they had participated, asking if we could do this again in the future. There were always several women who did not participate actively in the work-shops and who sat quietly or slept through them, and these tended to be women who were physically limited by their sight or were hard of hearing (although we used amplification); some were also not able to participate for cognitive reasons. However, we remember several women in particular who were positively affected by the workshops. Beulah in her 90s shared her poetry with the group, confident in her creativity. Esther who was 104 played the piano during lunch and asked for requests for songs from among the women present. Evelyn wanted to come to the second morning workshop but she was worried because it was her scheduled bath time, and she felt it couldn't possibly be changed. When we sug-gested that she had a choice here to negotiate a change, she fol-lowed through on this and did get her bath time changed. This small accomplishment in autonomy was extremely important to her, and in sharing this experience in self reliance she came to symbolize the potential of nursing home residents for self growth.

FRIENDSHIPS AND SOCIAL NETWORKS

One component of this project involved the coming-together and networking of women. Our goals included a fostering of interest and motivation in order to reduce isolation and depression among resident women; encouraging the individual sharing of experiences so that participants might see how these so-called individual prob-lems have structural causes and are shared by others; and also to allow for the possibility of women residents acting as advocates for each other both within and between institutions.

Research has demonstrated that many of the needs of institution-alized elderly for emotional support, companionship, advice, and guidance, can be met by informal social support networks that buffer the various stresses of aging and decrease the risk of illness and depression (Ell, 1984; Gallo, 1982; Pilisuk & Minkler, 1980). While there is much research done on the positive aspects of inter-generational contacts and friendships, kin generally, and even pets, on nursing home residents' life satisfactions (Hendy, 1987; Kocar-nik & Ponzetti, 1991; Seefeldt, 1987), there is less done on friend-ship patterns within the institution itself. However, as Retsinas and

Garrity (1985) suggest, there is "a lively social world" in nursing homes, and one that provides important social contacts for residents. Gutheil (1991) found that while nursing home friendships lacked in depth and intimacy, they provided companionship and support and played an important role in residents' emotional well-being. Similarly a study by Bitzan and Kruzich (1990) emphasized the importance of a close friend for resident participation in activities and satisfaction with life.

We found this to be true in working with the resident women. They talked about the importance of friendships and spoke generally about the pleasures and problems associated with roommates. They tended to have acquaintanceships and friendships that seemed less marked by class and life background and more by similarities associated with proximity (e.g., room location), age, and general levels of health. In several of the workshops, women from within the same nursing home were meeting each other for the first time, thus highlighting the relevance of proximity in friendship development.

Given the importance of friendship and social networks and the relevance of proximity for their development, we brought together women from different nursing homes, and provided a stimulating and comfortable environment where they could gather and meet each other. Food was crucial here, and most networking occurred over breakfast and lunch. The women were for the most part curious and interested to hear about life, rules, and goings-on in other nursing homes. It was an important experience for them to be able to identify with their home and compare it to perceptions of life and routines in the other homes. Most of the women with whom we worked hoped more workshops might be forthcoming and were on the whole most enthusiastic about the opportunity. Several recognized old friends from decades ago, and others spoke of family members and friends with whom they shared an acquaintance.

RESISTANCE AND CHANGE

The workshops were set up to provide opportunities for resident women to identify their feelings about the positive and negative aspects of their living situations and suggest areas for change. They were asked to envision the ideal nursing home and talk about what rules, if any, they would like to change. We told them that we would be sharing their suggestions (anonymously) with the staff in the afternoon staff training. The women worked in small groups with a designated note-taker and spokeswoman. We organized the groups so that there were opportunities for women from the same nursing homes to be together as well as mixing different women from different nursing homes.

Not surprisingly in terms of advantages, the women residents talked about the relief and "lack of worry" for them and their relatives associated with this living arrangement, the food and staff, and having company and activities to prevent loneliness. Yet these same issues were also discussed as sources of problems. Several stressed that while the staff were good they were always very busy and often preoccupied. Having company and people around also meant lack of privacy and the need to share bathrooms, and many remarked that the food wasn't cooked the way they would cook it or prefer it to be cooked. In these remarks the women emphasized their relative lack of autonomy and choice–about roommates, activities, food–and about their lack of personal possessions and sense of personal space. Many women spoke about the need for more personal space and would have liked "rooms of their own." They regretted the inability to have as many cherished possessions as they would like, and a familiar living space that they could really call home. Many alluded to the reality of theft in the nursing homes that prevented their wearing of rings, in particular, and other jewelry with which they had strong emotional attachment and fond memories. As studies have shown, residents with possessions appear better adapted to the institution since their possessions provide historical continuity, comfort, and a sense of belongingness (Wapner, Demick & Redondo, 1990).

The roommate issue seemed to come up a lot. Many women felt that this was an important area for change, and they wanted to have more control over roommate selection, suggesting "trial periods" of living together and a more careful selection procedure where roommates with similar interests might pair up. They emphasized that it was important for residents to be actively involved here in the decision making rather than be told the outcome. Again, central issues of autonomy were at stake, suggesting the need for intimacy balanced with a safe personal space in which boundaries were controlled by the women themselves. Several women articulated the need to be more "connected" and also suggested that they might help the staff with residents who needed more one-on-one direct care. Interestingly, while the residents described their need for intimate contacts, sex was never brought up as an issue. This probably reflected their modesty and well-socialized behavior as old women in this society.

Many residents stated that they would like more input in planning meaningful activities, including food preparation, which they felt was an important skill they had to offer. Meaningful activities for them included more of what we were doing in the workshop because it "made you think" and "helped us feel good about ourselves." Also a big emphasis was being able to "go places" and physically leave the nursing home. They were especially excited about being able to meet other women in similar circumstances, again highlighting the benefits of networking for psychosocial well-being. These women articulated the need to be active and useful in the nursing home community as well as to feel in control of their lives through exercising choice and autonomy. When we asked about their role in the residents' councils (mandated in many states as a way to encourage resident participation in administrative decision-making), we were met with mixed responses. Some women were involved and felt that their role was a positive one. Others were less enthusiastic saying that the resident males on the council dominated the meetings. Quite a few also said that they felt that their ideas were not taken seriously by administrators, and nothing really ever changed. Overall, however, we found that the residents who talked most about the lack of autonomy were those in the larger nursing homes where everyday life was more structured. Here their abilities to effect change through formal means such as the resident councils, and through more informal one-on-one ways, were more limited.

While for many the very idea of talking about "challenging" rules was a little improper, for others it gave them an opportunity to articulate frustrations and feelings they already had. Either way, they chuckled in mock horror at the thought of being asked to challenge rules and envision ideal nursing homes. During the large group discussion we discovered that while the particularities about roommates, food, bathrooms, and activities varied, the similarities centered on the importance of autonomy and control in establishing and maintaining human dignity. This is a crucial message for clinicians, administrators, and all those who work with the aged in institutional settings. One woman said at the beginning of an exercise on identifying choices within the structured confines of nursing home life: "If we had a choice, we wouldn't be here in the first place." Her statement was a poignant reminder.

WORKING WITH CAREGIVERS

Current literature emphasizes the crucial role of nursing home staff development (Burgio & Burgio, 1990; Hepler, 1987; Safford, 1991), and staff attitudes and ideological orientations to aging and the aged (Bagshaw & Adams, 1986; Chandler, Rachal & Kazelskis, 1986; Cohen-Marshfield, Rabinovich & Marx, 1991; Tellis-Nayak & Tellis-Nayak, 1989) in the maintenance of a healthy institution. In our attempt to help make the nursing homes a more supportive and hospitable environment for the growth of resident women's self reliance, and in the hopes of facilitating social change in the institution, we conducted three hour staff workshops at each site. These were very well attended by staff, including administrators and nursing and housekeeping personnel, and many received continuing education credit for their professional licensing.

In the training we focused on what we felt nursing home staff needed to learn and be reminded of, and what they identified as barriers to resident women's empowerment. As academics who were not in the nursing home on a daily basis, we were aware of being seen as out-of-touch "experts" and thus dismissed. With this in mind we spoke honestly of our respect for their work and the complexities and difficulties they might experience, and asked them to identify problem areas related to work as well as the kinds of support they needed in order to be effective in these roles. They cited institutional constraints and burn-out as the major problems and lack of recognition on the part of society, as well as lack of support, as immediate occupational problems and issues of concern.

In terms of our goals for staff development, we focused on the social construction of age and aging as a negative event in western society. We explored the sources and consequences of ageism as a system that discriminates and affects people of all ages, and the different contexts such as class, race and gender that affect these experiences. We asked the participants to imagine "what kind of an old woman/man they wanted to be," and then to consider the barriers to this vision as well as the changes that needed to happen in society in order for them to achieve the kind of experience they had described. This exercise attempted to get participants talking about how ageism is internalized, and how this might affect their relationships with the elderly, as well as foster an empathy and understanding toward residents, their "choices," and the need for change in society generally.

We shared our experiences of the residents' workshops, and our insights and techniques for self empowerment. Our discussion of reminiscence was especially well received, and we suggested that this might be expanded to include the use of short biographical "life reviews." These can be placed in the residents' charts and made available to staff as a way to challenge negative stereotyping about the elderly and personalize staff-resident interactions (Pietrukowicz & Johnson, 1991). Another idea comes courtesy of Judy Weisberg (1983) in her work with nursing home residents. With their consent, she displayed their biographies and photographs and publicly celebrated their unique strengths and experiences. She discusses the benefits of personalizing staff contributions in a similar way through attractive posters with artwork and photographs. She found this to have a positive effect on staff morale and enhanced self esteem and pride in work (Weisberg, 1988).

As we shared residents' suggestions for change, predictably many of these were met with dismay and resistance on the part of the staff. "It would be inefficient to . . ." or "it's impossible for us to . . ." etc., were common staff remarks. However, as a group we were able to highlight how institutional structures create parameters for interaction between staff and residents and institutionalize certain ways of doing things. We talked about wider systemic changes in the organization of health and nursing home services that needed to occur so that residents could have more control over their existence. Resident councils were emphasized as a place for residents to have some input, and we shared with the staff the residents' frustrations that "things didn't seem to change," as well as the domination of the councils by male residents. Important here then, is the need to see and use the resident councils as a place for respected input rather than as a token procedure that must be gone through before "business as usual." Fortunately there were several administrators present in the staff training who participated in these dialogues (albeit somewhat defensively at times) and who, we hope, left the workshops with some new information and insights.

CONCLUSION

In our work as clinicians and educators we can have an impact by acting as advocates for the improvement of the mental and material conditions of nursing home women residents' lives. We must emphasize how these two–the mental and the material–are so closely intertwined. Especially important here is the ability of women to have some control over the material conditions of their lives in the nursing home setting. With this in mind we can advocate for changes in several ways. First, we can work on ourselves in order to understand how issues of ageism and youth privilege interact with other social forces based upon gender, class, and race, and how our internalization of these issues affects our interaction with the old women in our lives. Dealing with these issues can help us to become better advocates for the improved psychosocial status of old women in nursing homes.

Second, as clinicians and educators we can work directly with resident women, recognizing that their continued invisibility is part of the overall problem. We can articulate their needs and celebrate their strengths and contributions. Projects such as the one shared here can start to help resident women feel better about themselves, reduce depression, and increase mental clarity and activity levels. Psychological well-being can increase dramatically when women residents are given opportunities for self reliance and autonomy, both through their participation in the ordering of their everyday lives and in the decision-making that affects the running of the institution. This is especially crucial for those whose psychological and/or physical health means that they are more vulnerable to institutional regimens. Also important here is the need for nursing home personnel to provide opportunities for formal and informal networking among resident women both within and between nursing homes, encouraging women to be advocates for each other.

Finally, as therapists and educators we can become advocates for women in nursing homes by working toward institutional changes that improve old women's status in society generally and in nursing homes in particular. Some changes to improve the material well-being of women residents include: the reduction of institutional size and increase in numbers of staff, the promotion of efforts for increased monetary remuneration, and recognition for lower-level nursing home personnel and staff development and training. Other beneficial changes involve the institutionalization of ombudspeople, resident councils, and other means for residents to have influence, and the creation of as many opportunities as possible for residents to increase their autonomy and take control of their lives.

We would like to close this essay with a section from the poem "After Sixty" by Marilyn Zuckerman (1988). Like "Warning," the women residents enjoyed and appreciated the bold declarations of autonomy and dignity contained in these lines.

> Everyone says the world is flat and finite
> on the other side of sixty
> That I will fall clear off the edge
> into darkness
>
> That no one will hear from me again or
> want to
>
> But I am ready for the knife slicing into the
> future
> for the quiet that explodes inside
> to join forces with the strong old woman
> to throw everything away and begin again . . .
>
> . . . There are places on this planet
> where women past the menopause
> put on the tribal robes
> smoke pipes of wisdom
> –fly

REFERENCES

Alexander, J., Berrow, D., Domitrovich, L., Donnelly, M., & McLean, C. (1986). *Women and aging: An anthology by women.* Corvallis, OR: Calyx Books.

Bagshaw, M., & Adams, M. (1986). Nursing home nurses' attitudes, empathy, and ideologic orientation. *International Journal of Aging and Human Development, 22*(3), 235-246.

Bitzan, J.E., & Kruzich, J.M. (1990). Interpersonal relationships of nursing home residents. *The Gerontologist, 30,* 385-390.

Brody, C.M. (1990). Women in a nursing home. *Psychology of Women Quarterly, 14,* 579-592.

Burgio, L.D., & Burgio, K.L. (1990). Institutional staff training and management: A review of the literature and a model for geriatric, long-term care facilities. *International Journal of Aging and Human Development, 30,* (4), 287-302.

Butler, R. (1963). The life-review: An interpretation of reminiscence in the aged. *Psychiatry, 26,* 65-76.

Chandler, J.T., Rachal, J.R. & Kazelskis, R. (1986). Attitudes of long-term care nursing personnel toward the elderly. *The Gerontologist, 26,* 551-555.

Cohen-Mansfield, J., Rabinovich, B.A. & Marx, M.C. (1991). Nurses' and social workers' perceptions of elderly nursing home residents' well-being. *Journal of Gerontological Social Work, 16,* (3/4), 135-147.

Cook, J.B. (1984). Reminiscing: How can it help confused nursing home residents? *Social Casework, 65,* 90-03.

Doress, P. & Siegal, D. (Eds.) (1988). *Ourselves growing older: Women aging with knowledge and power.* New York: Simon and Schuster.

Ell, K. (1984). Social networks, social support and health status: A review. *Social Service Review, 58,* 133-149.

Gallo, F. (1982). The effect of social support networks on the health of the elderly. *Social Work in Health Care, 8,* (2), 65-74.

Greenspan, M. (1983). *A new approach to women and therapy.* New York: McGraw Hill.

Gutheil, I.A. (1991). Intimacy in nursing home friendships. *Journal of Gerontological Social Work, 17,* (1/2), 59-73.

Hendy, H.M. (1987). Effects of pet and/or people visits on nursing home residents. *International Journal of Aging and Human Development, 25,* (4), 279-291.

Hepler, S.E. (1987). Assessing training needs for nursing home personnel. *Journal of Gerontological Social Work, 11,* (1/2), 71-79.

Joseph, J. (1987). Warning. In Martz, S. (Ed.), *When I am an old woman I shall wear purple* (p.1). Manhattan Beach, CA: Papier-Mache Press.

Kocarnik, R.A. & Ponzetti, J.J. (1991). The advantages and challenges of intergenerational programs in long term facilities. *Journal of Gerontological Social Work, 16,* (1/2), 97-107.

Koch, K. (1977). *I never told anyone: Teaching poetry in a nursing home.* New York: Random House.

Lyman, A.J. & Edwards, M.E. (1989). Poetry and life-review for frail American-Indian elderly. *Journal of Gerontological Social Work, 14*, (1/2), 75-91.

McDermott, C.J. (1989). Empowering the elderly nursing home resident: the resident rights campaign. *Social Work, 34*, 155-157.

MacDonald, B. & Rich, C. (1983). *Look me in the eye.* San Francisco: Spinsters/ Aunt Lute.

Merriam, S.B. (1989). The structure of simple reminiscence. *The Gerontologist, 29*, (6), 761-767.

One Fine Day (film) (1984). Produced by Martha Wheelock and Kay Weaver, distrib. Circe Records, 256 S. Robertson Blvd., Beverly Hills, CA 90211 and Ishtar Films, Rt.311, Patterson, N.Y. 12563.

Perschbacher, R. (1984). The application of reminiscence in an activity setting. *The Gerontologist, 24*, 343-345.

Pietrukowicz, M.E., & Johnson, M.S. (1991). Using life histories to individualize nursing home staff attitudes toward residents. *The Gerontologist, 31*, 102-106.

Pilisuk, M., & Minkler, M. (1980). Supportive networks: Life ties for the elderly. *Journal of Social Issues, 3*, (6), 95-116.

Rattenbury, C., & Stones, M.J. (1989). A controlled evaluation of reminiscences and current topics discussion groups in a nursing home context. *The Gerontologist, 29*, 68-71.

Retsinas, J., & Garrity, P. (1985). Nursing home friendships. *The Gerontologist, 25*, 376-381.

Romaniuk, M.R. (1983). The application of reminiscence to the clinical interview. *Clinical Gerontologist, 1*, 39-43.

Russell, C. (1987). Aging as a feminist issue. *Women's Studies International Forum, 10*, (2), 125-132.

Ruth Stout's Garden (film) (1976). Arthur Mokin Productions.

Seefeldt, C. (1987). The effects of preschoolers' visits to a nursing home. *The Gerontologist, 27*, 228-232.

Smyer, M.A. (1989). Nursing homes as a setting for psychological practice: Public policy perspectives. *American Psychologist, 44*: 1307-1314.

Safford, F. (1991). 'If you don't like the care, why don't you take your mother home?' Obstacles to family/staff partnerships in the institutional care of the aged. *Journal of Gerontological Social Work, 13*, (3/4), 1-7.

Sturdivant, S. (1980). *Therapy with women: A feminist philosophy of treatment.* New York: Springer.

Taft, L.B., & Nehrke, M.F. (1990). Reminiscence, life review, and ego integrity in nursing home residents. *International Journal of Aging and Human Development, 30*, (3), 189-196.

Tellis-Nayak, V., & Tellis-Nayak, M. (1989). Quality of care and the burden of two cultures: when the world of the nurses' aide enters the world of the nursing home. *The Gerontologist, 29*, 307-313.

Wapner, S., Demick, J. & Redondo, J.P. (1990). Cherished possessions and adaptation of older people to nursing homes. *International Journal of Aging and Human Development, 31*, (3), 219-235.

Weisberg, J. (1983). Raising self-esteem of mentally impaired nursing home residents. *Social Work, 28*, 163-164.

_____ (1988). Fostering self esteem in nursing home staff. *Social Work, 33*, 62.

Wells, L.M., & Singer, C. (1985). A model for linking networks in social work practice with the institutionalized elderly. *Social Work, 30*, 318-322.

Young-Eisendrath, P., & Weidemann, F. (1987). *Female authority: Empowering women through psychotherapy.* New York: Guildford Press.

Zuckerman, M. (1988). After sixty. In Doress, P. & Siegal, D. (Eds.), Ourselves growing older: Women aging with knowledge and power (p. 405). New York: Simon and Schuster.